Stepping Up To Fluency 2

A Systematic Stuttering Therapy Program for SLPs

Janice Pechter Ellis

Dedication

To my loving husband, Howard

my partner in life, and my best friend

Copyright©2017 by Janice Pechter Ellis

All rights reserved.

Permission is granted for the user to reproduce pages so indicated in limited form for instructional use only.

No other parts of this book may be reproduced or transmitted in any form or by any means, electronic or mechanical, including photocopying and recording, or by any information storage and retrieval system, without written permission from the author.

Published by:

Shelden Studios
PO Box 3221
Prince Frederick, MD 20678

ISBN 978-0-9977147-1-5

Printed in the United States of America
by INGRAM / Lightning Source, Inc.

Stepping Up to Fluency 2
Table of Contents

Introduction 5
   Target Behaviors 5
   Program Components 5
   The Fluency Criterion 6

Baseline Charting 7
   Disfluency Rate Baseline Charts: Levels I and II 7
   Syllable Rate Baseline Charts: Level I 8
   Sample Baseline Charts: Level I 9
   Reproducible Charts 10-11
   Level I Clients' Sample Charts 12-17
   Syllable Rate Baseline Charts: Level II 18
   Sample Baseline Charts: Level II 19
   Conversation Mode 19
   Level II Clients' Sample Charts 20-24
   Selection of Material to Elicit Baseline Samples 25
   Eye Contact 25

The Identification Stage 26
   Defining Stuttering Behaviors 26
   Teaching Level I Clients to Identify Disfluencies 27-28
   Teaching Level II Clients to Identify Disfluencies 29

Target Training 30
   Target Definitions: Level I 31
   Target Definitions: Level II 32
   Full Breath 33
   Easy Onset 34-37
   Continuous Speech 38-40
   Easy Onset Phrases, Questions and Sentences – Level I 41-44
   Easy Onset Phrases, Questions and Sentences – Level II 45-48
   Light Contact 49
   The Speech Helpers 50-51
   Light Contact Words 52-55
   Strategies for Sounds Other than Plosives 56
   Multisyllabic Words: Level II 56-57

Practice Pages 58-59
   Stepping up to Fluency 2 Score Sheet 60-61
   Practice Pages: Level I 62-65
   Practice Pages: Level II 66-71
   Multisyllabic Words in Short Sentences: Level II 72
   The Final Target — **Phrasing** 73
   Determining the Placement of Slash Marks and Procedures 74-75

Stepping Up to Fluency 2 - Table of Contents, *continued*

Stories for Phrasing Practice: Level I	76-78
Stories for Phrasing Practice: Level II	79-81
Use of Poems for Phrasing Practice	82-91
Use of Intermittent Slash Marks	92
Stories with Intermittent Slash Marks: Level I	93-96
Complex Easy Onset Sentences with Multisyllabic Words Worksheet	97
Stories with Intermittent Slash Marks: Level II	98-103
The Fluency Targets Quiz	104-105

Activities for Conversation, Carryover, and Maintenance 106
    Promoting Fluency in Conversation 106
    Suggested activities for Carryover 107-110
    Maintenance 110

Picture Cards 111
    Practice Pictures [p], [b], [t], [d], [k], [g] 113-124
    Mr. Yes and Mr. No 125

About the Author 126

List of Reproducible Pages

Disfluency Rate Baseline Chart	10
Syllable Rate Baseline Chart	11
Target Definitions	31-32
Easy Onset Words and Curve	36-37
Continuous Speech	38-40
Easy Onset Phrases, Questions and Sentences – Level I	41-44
Easy Onset Phrases, Questions and Sentences – Level II	45-48
The Speech Helpers	51
Light Contact Words	53-55
Multisyllabic Words	57
Stepping up to Fluency 2 Score Sheet	61
Practice Pages: Level I	62-65
Practice Pages: Level II	66-71
Multisyllabic Words in Short Sentences: Level II	72
Stories for Phrasing Practice: Level I	76-78
Stories for Phrasing Practice: Level II	79-81
Poems for Phrasing Practice	83-91
Stories with Intermittent Slash Marks: Level I	93-96
Complex Easy Onset Sentences with Multisyllabic Words	97
Stories with Intermittent Slash Marks: Level II	98-103
The Fluency Targets Quiz	105
Practice Pictures	113-124
Mr. Yes and Mr. No	125
About the Author	126

Introduction

Stepping Up to Fluency 2 is designed for use by speech-language pathologists treating children and adults who stutter. This innovative program teaches stuttering clients to produce consistently fluent speech in an average of 25 sessions in Level I clients (kindergarten through approximately third grade) and 30-35 sessions for Level II clients (at or about fourth grade through adult).

Its primary goal is to develop and maintain fluent speech in a variety of speaking tasks and environments using five specific clinical targets. It includes methods, worksheets, stories, and poems that are invaluable tools for use with kindergarten through adult clients. The stimulus sheets and activities reflect the different interests and reading levels of the two age levels.

This program is the result of the author's 40 years of working with stutterers ages 4 through 51 in both school based and private practice. The author's clinical skills evolved from participation in the Precision Fluency Shaping Program designed by Ronald Webster, PhD., and utilized in the 1970's at the Walter Reed Army Medical Center, Washington D.C.; and the fluency program at the George Washington University, under the direction of James W. Hillis, PhD.; as well as application of Dr. Bruce P. Ryan's work on operant analysis, establishment, maintenance, and transfer programs.

Target Behaviors

Helping clients develop and maintain fluent speech in a variety of speaking tasks is accomplished by retraining breathing, awareness of articulators, production of vowels and consonants, and phrasing. Each client is required to recognize, develop, and perfect five target behaviors:

- *Using a Full Breath* to sustain a short sentence
- *Easy Onset* for initiating sounds for words beginning with vowels
- *Continuous Speech* to eliminate "choppy" pauses between words
- *Light Contact* when producing initial consonant sounds
- *Phrasing* groups of words together by meaning or syntactic boundaries

This process helps clients understand their own disfluencies and develop systematic strategies for managing them.

Program Components

Recordkeeping Charts

Stepping Up to Fluency 2 includes reproducible Disfluency Rate and Syllable Rate Baseline Charts (pages 10 and 11) to monitor the client's progress. The client's rate of disfluencies in two-minute monologue and reading exercises should be charted at the beginning of each treatment session. The client strives to bring the graph for disfluencies per minute down to the "zero line." Regular charting of the client's performance at the beginning of each treatment session provides systematic reinforcement and feedback for the client, clinician, and parents. Charting syllable per minute rates in monologues and readings is recommended if time permits. Brief profiles and charts of several clients are included.

Practice Worksheets

The first four fluency target behaviors are presented using the reproducible definitions and stimulus lists in this manual. After the client learns basic target behaviors, Practice Pages 1-4 (for Level I and Level II clients) which contain commonly used words and phrases are introduced. Using these worksheets, clients learn to choose which targets to use to overcome their disfluencies.

Picture Cards

Stepping Up to Fluency 2 contains 72 black and white line drawings in reproducible worksheets and flash cards. Light contact targets can be practiced with these stimuli; nonreaders can use them instead of reading the lists of stimulus words for this target.

Stories and Poems

Twelve stories and nine pages of poems are provided for instruction of the Phrasing target. These materials are grouped according to reading ability and interest level of Level I and Level II clients.

The Speech Book

Every client is given a folder at the onset of treatment to serve as a "speech book" to keep copies of baseline charts, definitions of the five target skills, and practice worksheets. This folder becomes a workbook filled with explanations and exercises as the program progresses. For school-based clients, the client's name, the word SPEECH, and the day and time of the scheduled session or sessions may be written on the cover. The speech book can also serve as a hall pass (depending on school policy) and help the child remember to come on time. The more importance the clinician places on the speech book, the more importance it has for the client. Part of the client's responsibility is bringing the folder with charts and practice sheets intact to each session. This process also enables the parents to take part in all practice exercises and maintain a dialogue with the SLP regarding progress.

The Fluency Criterion

The program's design encourages clients to speak with precision at every level of training. Once the identification stage is complete and training has begun, a client progresses to the next higher level of difficulty only when complete fluency has been attained at the current level. For the purposes of this program, a client must achieve 100% accurate uses of fluency targets on a given worksheet without a model to progress to the next task.

> A client may be dismissed from the program after maintaining less than or equal to one disfluency or stuttered syllable per minute on reading and monologue baseline charts for ten consecutive sessions and after completing several carryover activities.

Baseline Charting

For complete success in this program, the evaluation of client progress must be objective, consistent, and ongoing. Required disfluency per minute and optional syllable per minute rates should be sampled on a weekly basis using the baseline charts provided on pages 10 and 11. These charts give immediate feedback to the client at the beginning of each session.

Using a stopwatch and tape recording device (tape or digital recorder) to take baseline samples is recommended to ensure reliability and validity of the baseline scores. The tape recorder is essential to compute syllable per minute rates. Tape recording the baseline samples also facilitates the treatment process for both the client and the clinician; the recording later can provide positive feedback to show the client's progress.

Disfluency Rate Baseline Charts: Levels I and II

Ongoing Disfluency Rate Baseline Charts should be kept for monologue and reading (if the client is able to read) for all clients, regardless of treatment setting. This is a requirement for the *Stepping Up to Fluency 2* program. At the beginning of every session, the client should talk and read for a set time interval (usually two minutes for each). While the client provides these baseline samples, the clinician should give no reminders about specific fluency techniques other than "use your best speech" or "remember your targets" at the beginning of the sampling.

Clinicians then tally the number of disfluencies the client experiences while reading or talking, and write specific examples, such as:

- "boys" [block]
- "go" [part-word repetition]
- "I want" [phrase repetition]

using their own shorthand or abbreviations for different types of disfluencies. Care should be taken counting disfluencies that appear to be due to reading or linguistic formulation errors. Some clients can provide feedback regarding which disfluencies are reading mistakes and which are actual instances of stuttering.

Quickly discuss those instances of stuttering identified, allowing the client to tell which type each disfluency was. Then, record the data on two sets of charts, one for the file and one for the client's speech book. To make the charts more readable, keep separate charts for reading and monologue data or use different color ink to track each mode, such as red for reading and green for monologue. Even young clients eagerly look at their charts each session to see how close their scores are to the "zero line." These charts are visual, objective progress reports which provide positive and negative reinforcement and motivation for the client. Current baseline data should be recorded and the charts reviewed with the client as a regular part of each session.

Syllable Rate Baseline Charts: *Level I*

The initial evaluation for a client who stutters should include:

- Syllable per minute calculation for both reading and monologue samples
- Disfluency per minute count

Evaluation and regular monitoring of syllable rate is important in a comprehensive fluency program for several reasons. A stutterer's rate can affect fluency negatively if the rate is excessively rapid (faster than 200 syllables per minute in young children). On the other hand, an individual's rate may be affected adversely by the stuttering. Because of actual blocks, prolongations, and repetitions, the speech-phonation time becomes significantly less than the speech-attempted time, causing an unusually slow rate (80 to 100 syllables per minute). Other stutterers' rates may be unaffected by their disfluencies. An example of this is client R.M. on page 17. The syllable per minute rate at the onset of treatment was acceptable and needed no intervention. However, rates were charted periodically for precise monitoring, and his rate did increase slightly as he became more fluent.

A large discrepancy between the reading rates and speaking rates of very young children is typical The reading rate will be much slower because reading is a newly acquired skill. This is apparent on the Syllable Rate Baseline Chart for client A.C. on page 15. His reading rate varied between 80 syllables per minute and 130 syllables per minute initially. By the eleventh session, his reading rate began to stabilize at 110 syllables per minute while fluency rates on page 14 remained equal to or less than one disfluency per minute.

The rate of speaking must be considered when planning treatment goals; one goal might be to modify the client's syllable rate along with the disfluency rate. Variation in individual performance also should be considered in evaluating speech rate; individual syllable rates can vary widely. Intervention is appropriate only if the rate affects, or is affected by, the individual's disfluency. Appropriate syllable per minute goals can be determined after four or five sessions with the client. Average syllable per minute rates collected during several sessions determine whether to intervene with speech rate because they provide a more accurate impression of the client's overall speech rate. Speech rate goals can be changed later if they become unrealistic for a client.

Periodic syllable per minute checks are important even if the client's initial speech rate is appropriate because the rate can change as the client becomes more fluent. In clinical settings, computing syllable per minute rates after each session is recommended. If syllable rates increase as the client's speech becomes more fluent, rates should be monitored closely in case the client begins to speak too quickly and lose sight of the targets. This is called *riding on fluency* and must be avoided at all costs.

Syllable rate intervention generally consists of nothing more than making the client (and parent, if appropriate) aware of the problem by pointing out trends shown on the charts. Having family members practice a slower speech model for the child to follow in general conversation is helpful. Awareness of the problem and slower speech models usually stimulate self-correction.

Sample Baseline Charts: *Level I*

Sample baseline charts for three clients are provided on the following pages. They show the number of disfluencies per minute and number of syllables per minute in monologue and reading tasks.

Client D.S., a five-year-old male nonreader, was seen individually for one hour per week for 22 sessions. His charts include an in-session baseline chart for a two-minute monologue. There is a chart for disfluencies and one for syllable count.

Client A.C., a six-year-old male, also was seen individually for one hour per week. His charts include in-session baseline charts for reading and monologue. He completed the program in 23 sessions. A.C. maintained the criterion of no more than one disfluency per minute during baseline measures for seven consecutive weeks, rather than the ten usually required for dismissal. Once he completed the maintenance portion of the program, he was dismissed.

Client R.M., an eight-year-old male, was a public school client seen in a small group twice per week. In-session charts for reading and monologue are provided. He completed the program in 31 sessions.

Disfluency Rate Baseline Chart

Client _____ Chart No. _____ Age _____ Sex _____ Clinician _____

Environment _____ Listener _____ Goals: *Disf./Min.* _____ *Duration* _____

SESSION #	DATE	DISFLUENCIES PER MINUTE
1		
2		
3		
4		
5		
6		
7		
8		
9		
10		
11		
12		
13		
14		
15		
16		
17		
18		
19		
20		
21		
22		
23		
24		
25		
26		
27		
28		
29		
30		
31		
32		
33		
34		
35		
36		
37		
38		

Scale: 5, 10, 15, 20

MODE: ☐ Reading ●   ☐ Monologue ▲   ☐ Conversation ◆

Stepping Up to Fluency 2. Copyright © 2017 by Janice Pechter Ellis. This page may be reproduced for individual instructional use only.

Syllable Rate Baseline Chart

Client		Chart No.	Age	Sex	Clinician
Environment	Listener	Goals: *Syll./Min.*			*Duration*

SESSION #	DATE	SYLLABLES PER MINUTE 100　　　　　150　　　　　200　　　　　250　　　　　290
1		
2		
3		
4		
5		
6		
7		
8		
9		
10		
11		
12		
13		
14		
15		
16		
17		
18		
19		
20		
21		
22		
23		
24		
25		
26		
27		
28		
29		
30		
31		
32		
33		
34		
35		
36		
37		
38		

MODE:　　☐ Reading ●　　　　☐ Monologue ▲　　　　☐ Conversation ◆

Stepping Up to Fluency 2. Copyright © 2017 by Janice Pechter Ellis. This page may be reproduced for individual instructional use only.

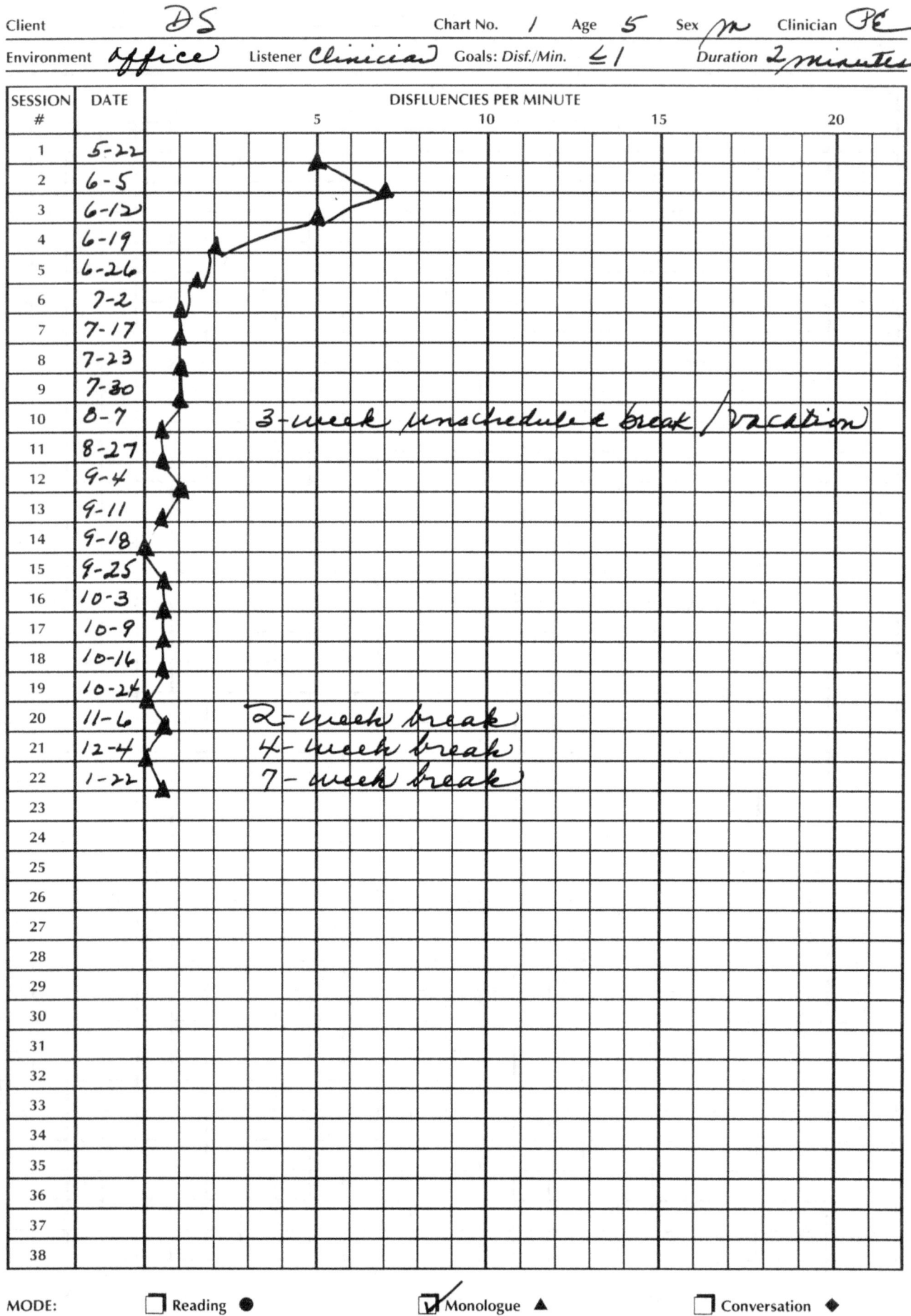

Syllable Rate Baseline Chart

Client: DS Chart No. 1 Age 5 Sex m Clinician PE
Environment: Office Listener: Clinician Goals: Syll./Min. ▲ 125-150 Duration 2 min.

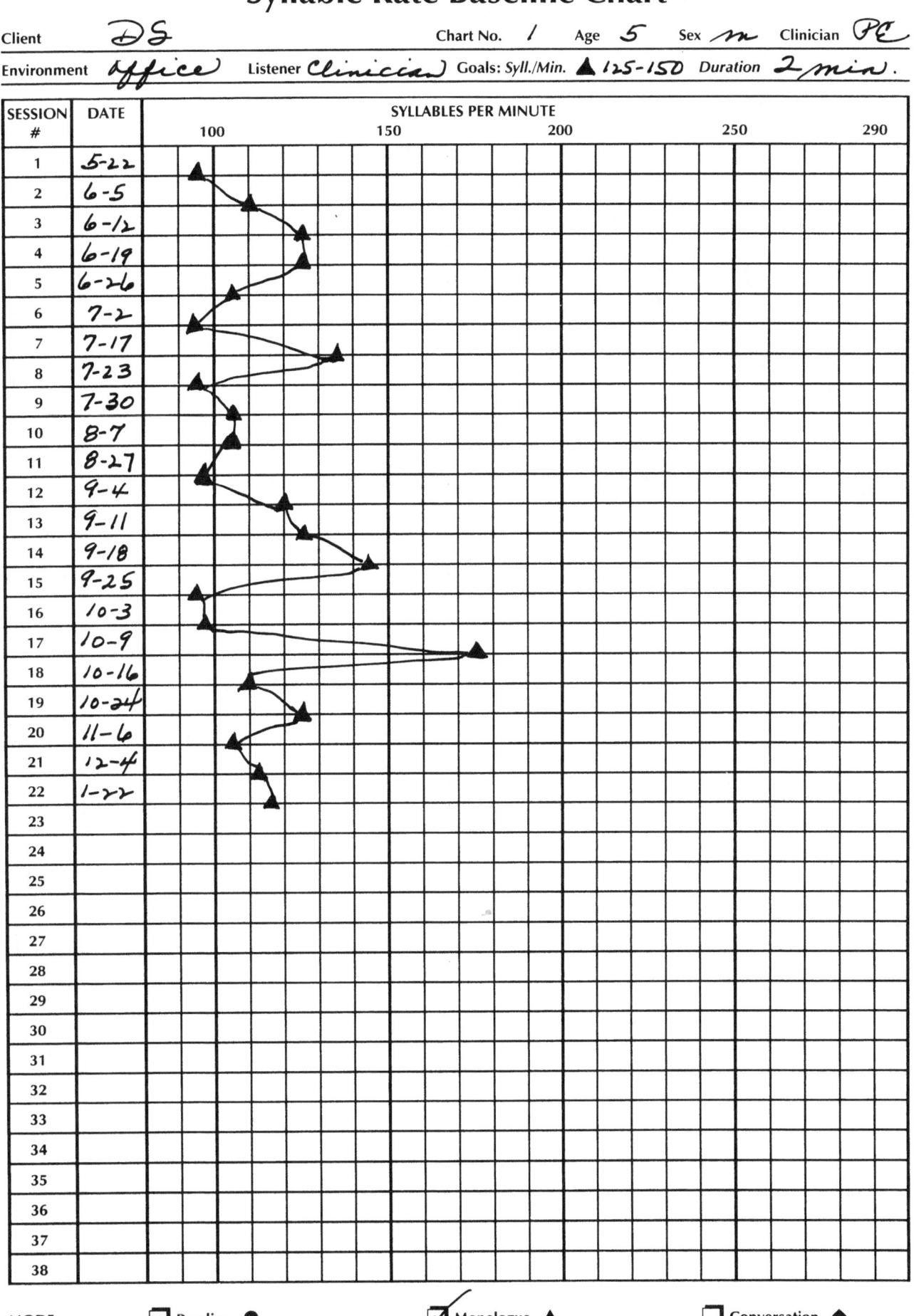

MODE: ☐ Reading ●   ☑ Monologue ▲   ☐ Conversation ◆

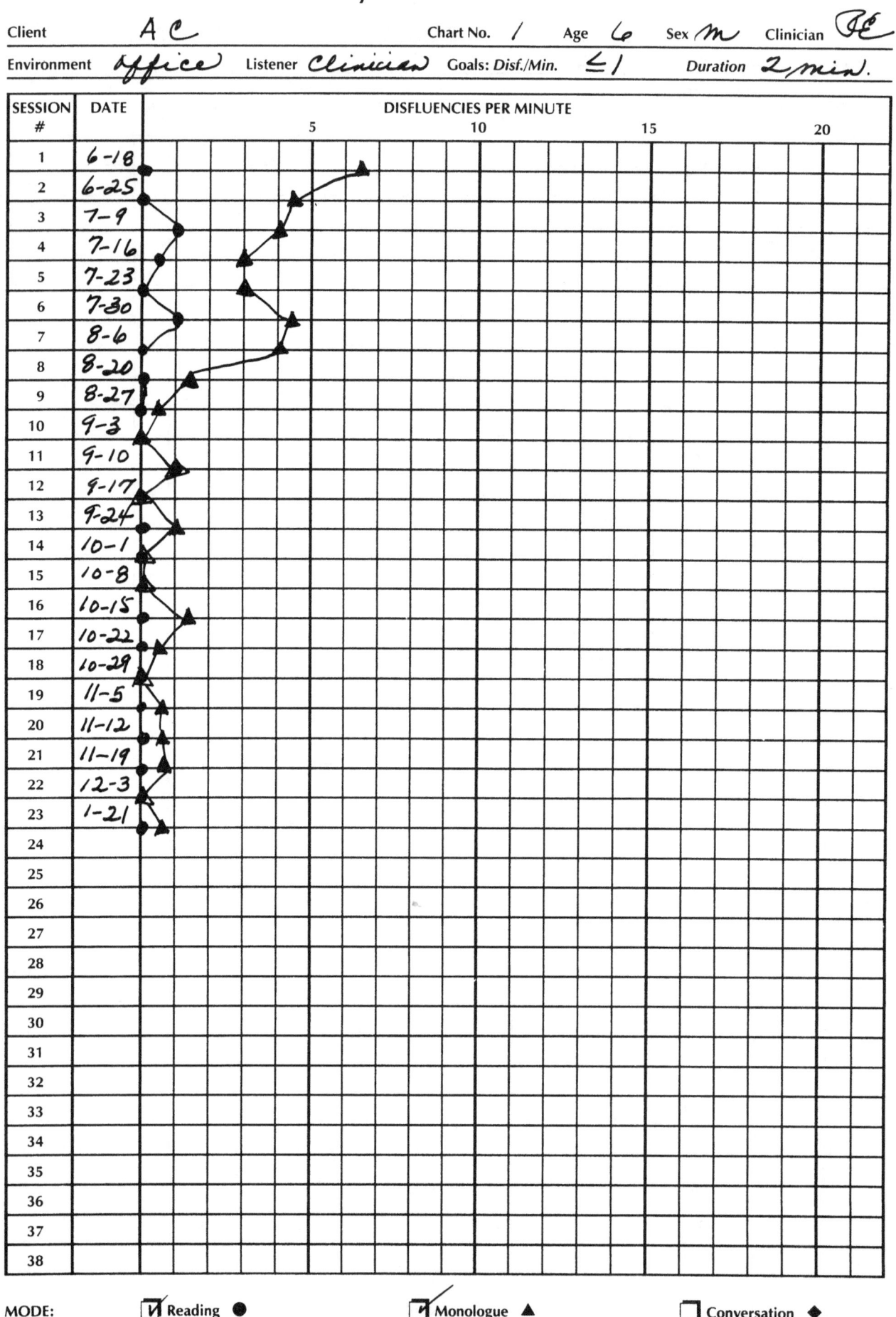

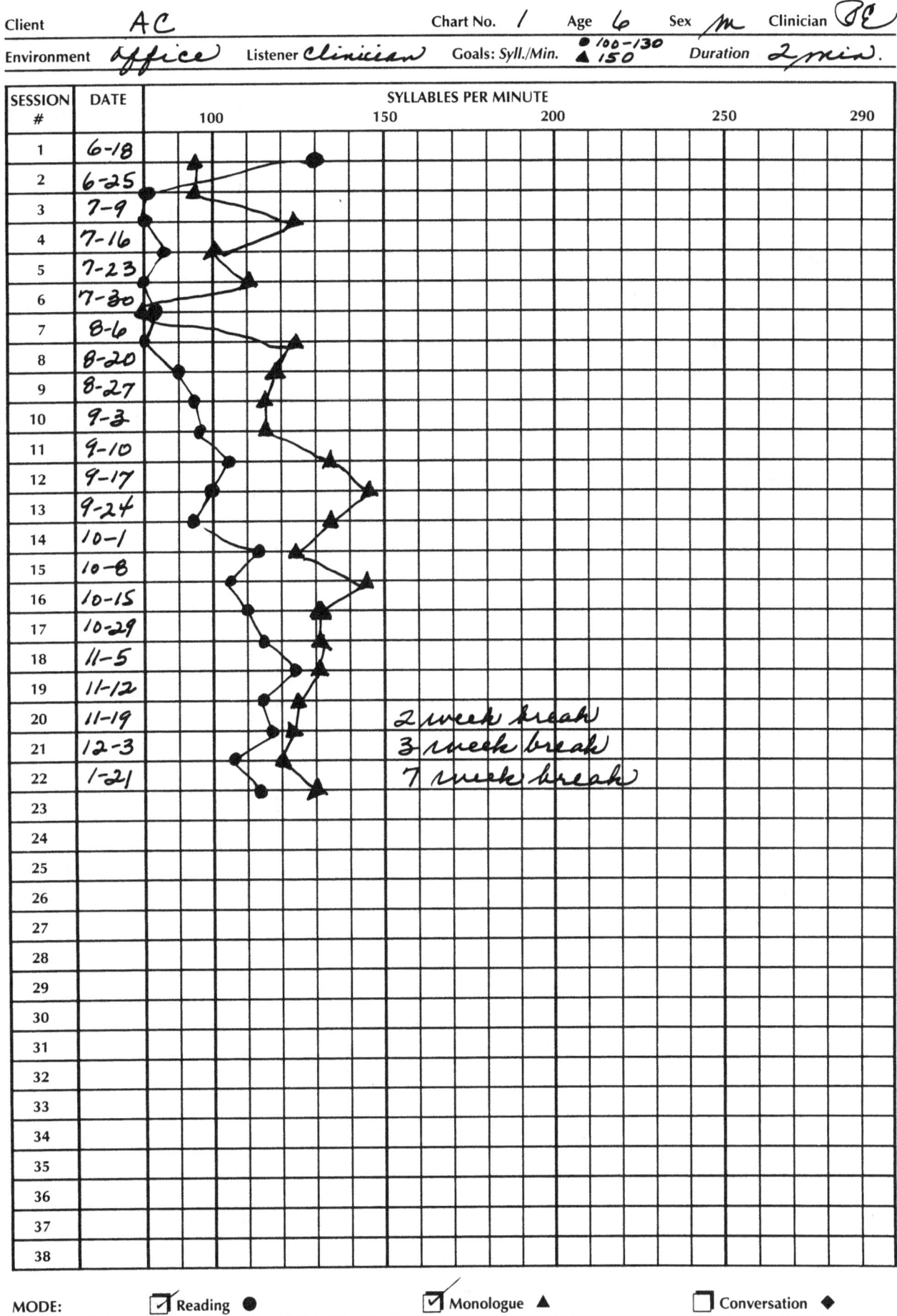

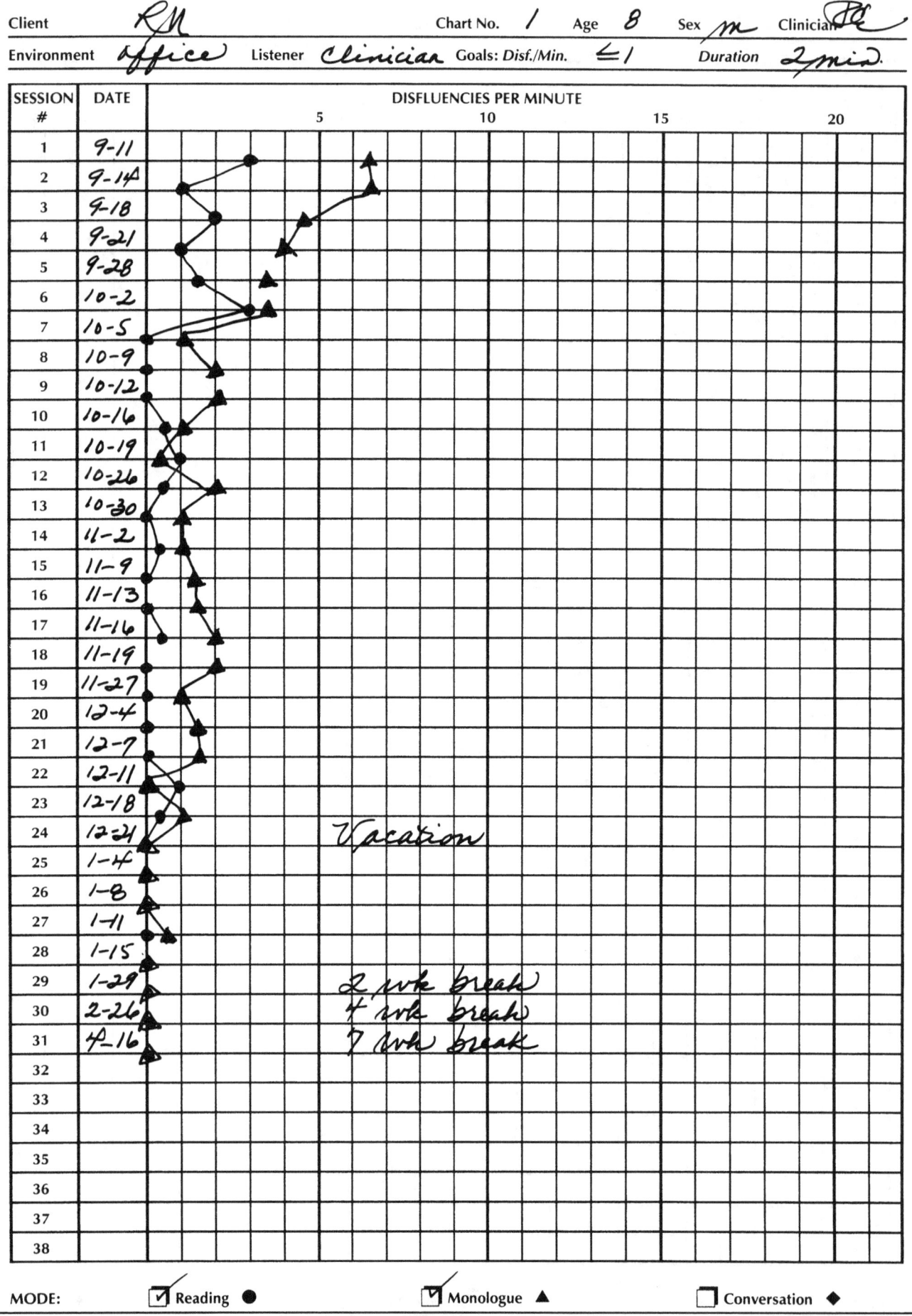

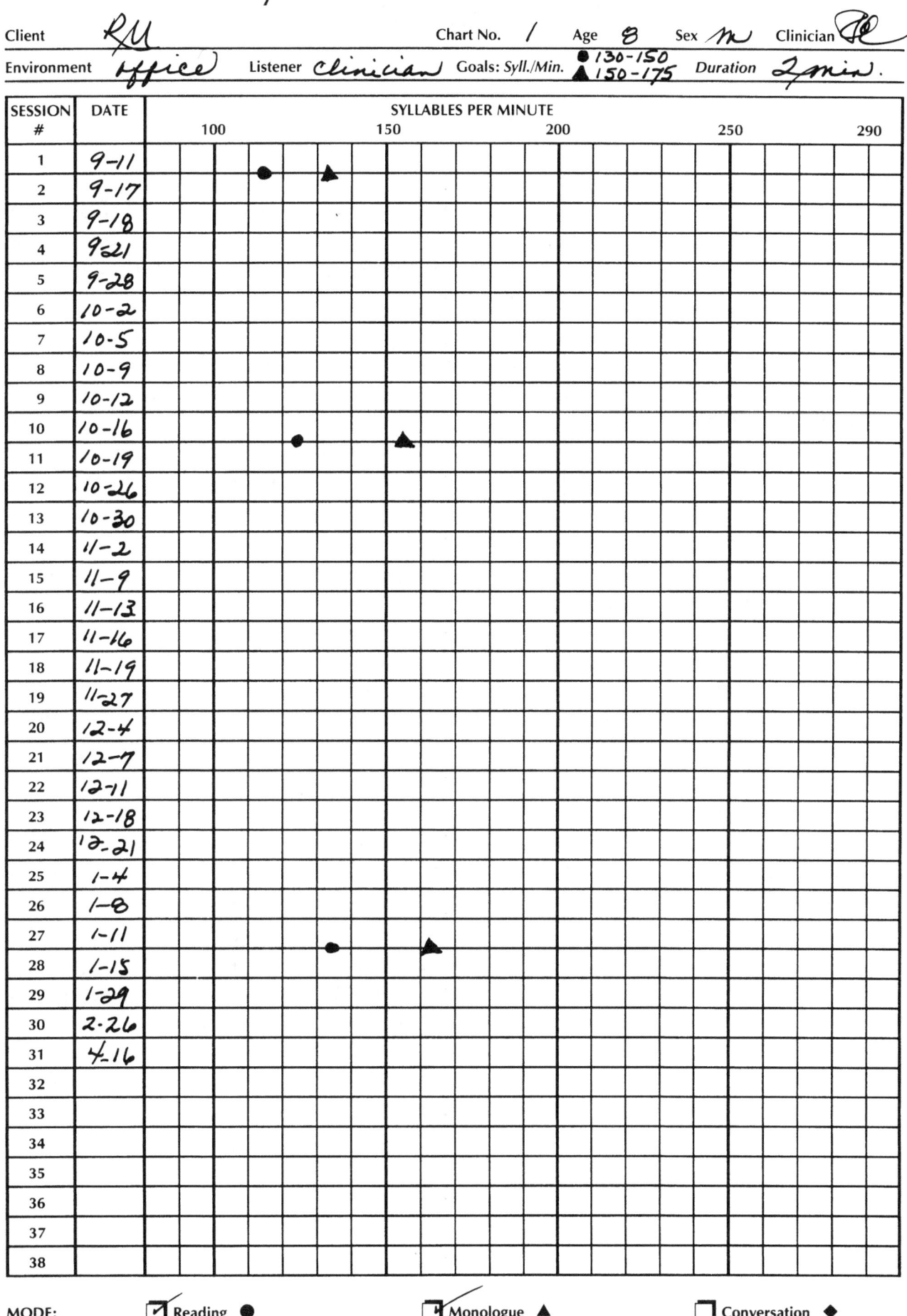

Syllable Rate Baseline Charts: Level II

The initial evaluation for a client who stutters should include two calculations for both reading and monologue performance:

- Syllable per minute count
- Disfluency per minute count

A stutterer's rate can affect fluency negatively if the rate is excessively rapid (faster than 225 syllables per minute). On the other hand, an individual's rate may be affected adversely by the stuttering. Because of actual blocks, prolongations, and repetitions, the speech-phonation time becomes significantly less than the speech-attempted time, causing an unusually slow rate (100-125 syllables per minute).

These elements must be considered when planning goals; if needed, work may be done on both the client's syllable rate and the disfluency rate. Syllable rate intervention generally consists of making the client (or the parents of a school age child) aware of the problem by pointing out trends on the charts. This awareness usually stimulates self-correction. Allowing for individual differences is important; syllable rates vary widely in different people. Intervention should occur only if the rate affects or is affected by the disfluency.

If the client's syllable rate is inappropriate (generally, greater than 225 syllables per minute or less than 125 syllables per minute), this rate should be charted on a regular basis. In many instances, the syllable rate corrects itself as the disfluency rate approaches the zero point for that mode. Client A.G.'s Syllable Rate Chart on page 21 shows his monologue rate at the onset of treatment was 100 syllables per minute. By the tenth session, his rate had risen to 178 syllables per minute without direct intervention.

When syllable rates increase as clients become more fluent, the rate should be monitored closely because they may use an excessively fast rate and lose sight of the targets. This *riding on fluency* should be avoided. In contrast, the rates of other stutterers may be unaffected by their disfluencies. An example is client K.R. whose syllable per minute rate at the onset of treatment on page 23 was acceptable and needed no intervention. However, they were charted periodically for precise monitoring.

For these reasons, the charting of syllable rates is important in a comprehensive program although sometimes it may not be possible. One solution to this problem is periodic syllable per minute checks. This should be decided for each individual case although computing syllable per minute counts for each session is recommended.

Sample Baseline Charts: Level II

Sample baseline charts for two clients are provided. Client A.G., a 16 year, one-month-old male, was seen individually one hour per week for 32 sessions. His charts include in-session baseline charts for disfluencies and syllables. He was dismissed from treatment following a final review session one month later.

Client K.R., male, 15 years old, was seen at his high school twice a week for a total of 30 sessions, then once a week for the final four sessions before the end of the school year. His last four sessions were held in autumn with no sessions held during summer vacation. These sessions were spaced four weeks apart for the maintenance stage of the treatment program.

Conversation Mode

To chart the conversation mode: Once the client reaches carryover activities in the program, the conversation mode should be charted. At this time, determination of whether the client will chart phone calls, interviews, and conversations with coworkers, friends, or teachers should be made (syllables per minute are not computed for this goal). Before carryover activities are begun, the client should maintain equal to or less than one disfluency per minute in both reading and monologue tasks for at least ten consecutive sessions to show in-session fluency has stabilized.

Disfluency Rate Baseline Chart

Client: AG Chart No. 1 Age 16-1 Sex M Clinician PE
Environment: office Listener: clinician Goals: Disf./Min. ≤ 1 Duration: 2 minutes

Session #	Date
1	9-2
2	9-9
3	9-16
4	9-23
5	9-30
6	10-8
7	10-14
8	10-21
9	10-28
10	11-4
11	11-11
12	11-18
13	11-29
14	12-9
15	12-16
16	12-21
17	12-30
18	1-6
19	1-13
20	1-20
21	1-26
22	2-10
23	2-17
24	2-24
25	3-3
26	3-10
27	3-17
28	3-24
29	4-7
30	4-21
31	4-28
32	5-12

MODE: ☑ Reading ●   ☑ Monologue ▲   ☐ Conversation ◆

20

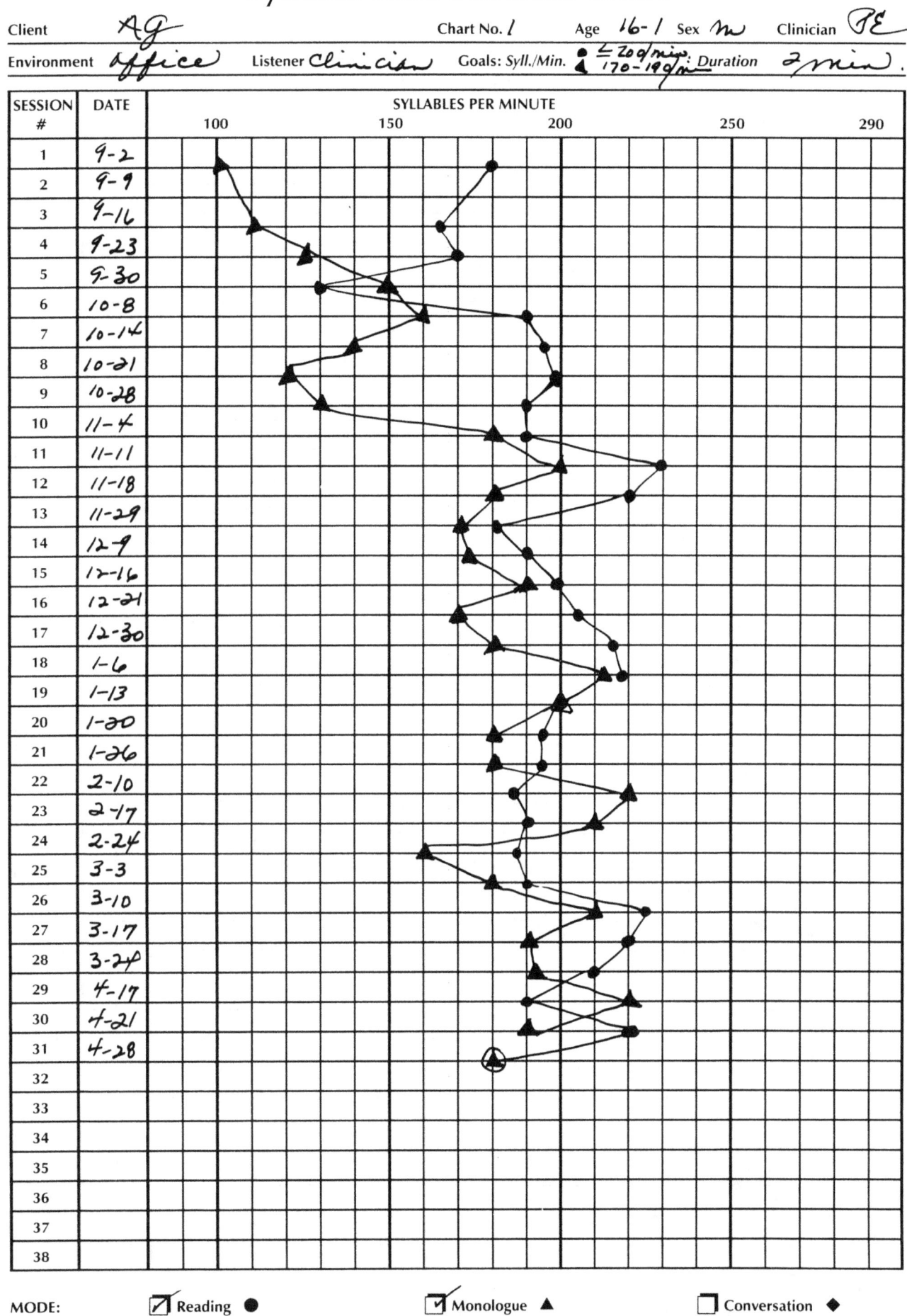

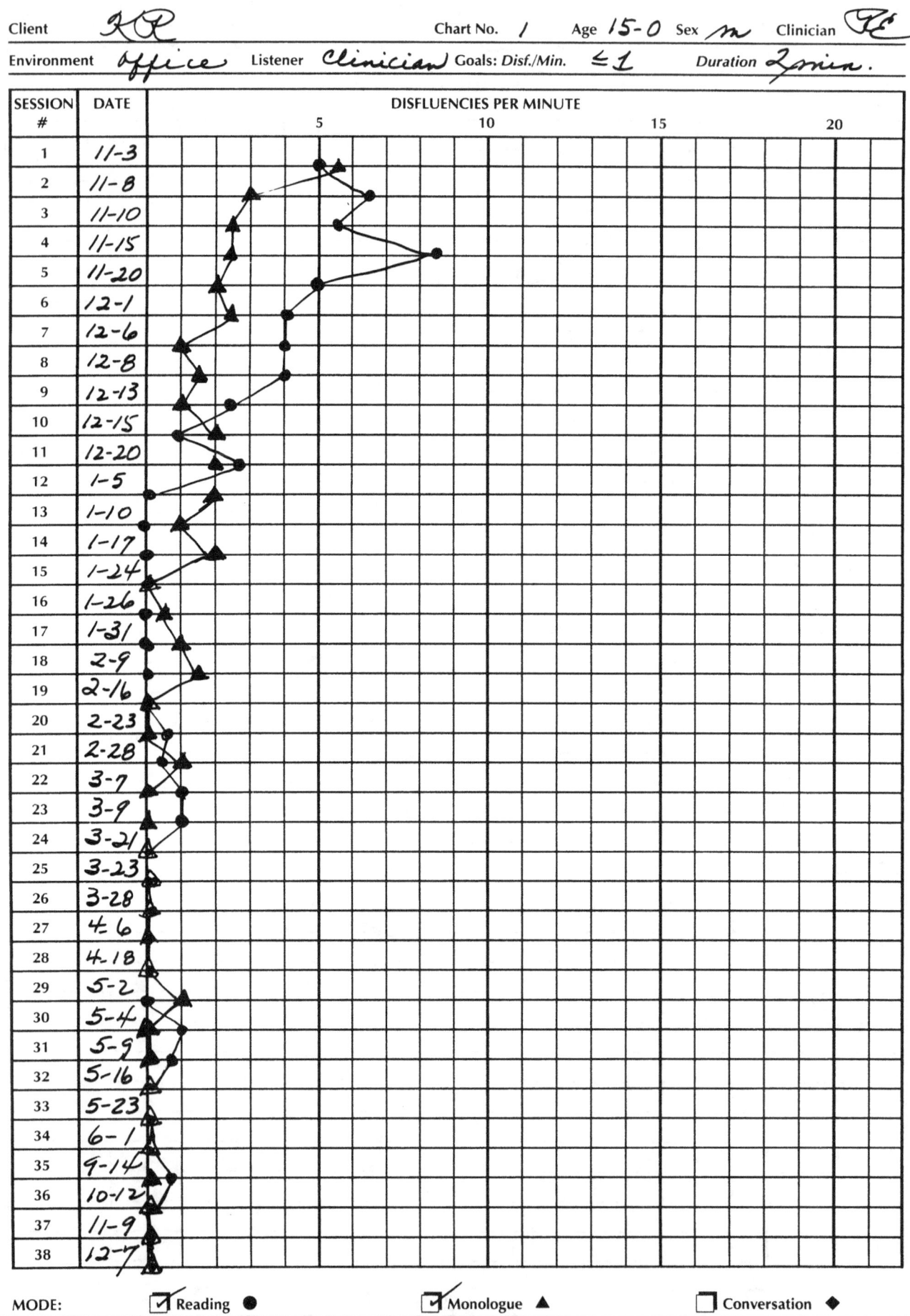

Syllable Rate Baseline Chart

Client: KR Chart No. 1 Age: 15-0 Sex: M Clinician: RE
Environment: office Listener: Clinician Goals: Syll./Min. ≤1 Duration: 2 min.

SESSION #	DATE	SYLLABLES PER MINUTE (100 — 150 — 200 — 250 — 290)
1	11-3	▲ at ~185, ● at ~200
2		
3		
4		
5		
6		
7		
8		
9		
10		
11		
12		
13		
14		
15		
16		
17		
18	2-9	▲ at ~185, ● at ~200
19		
20		
21		
22		
23		
24		
25		
26		
27		
28	4-18	▲ at ~185, ● at ~190
29		
30		
31		
32		
33		
34		
35		
36		
37		
38		

MODE: ☑ Reading ●   ☑ Monologue ▲   ☐ Conversation ◆

Disfluency Rate Baseline Chart

Client: KR Chart No. 2 Age: 15-0 Sex: M Clinician: FE
Environment: School Listener: Staff, Clerks Goals: Disf./Min. ≤1 Duration: Varied

SESSION #	DATE	DISFLUENCIES PER MINUTE
1	5-9	Telephoning music store
2	5-16	" " Sports store
3	5-23	Interviewing school security officer
4	6-1	" " vice principal
5		
6		
7		
8		
9		
10		
11		
12		
13		
14		
15		
16		
17		
18		
19		
20		
21		
22		
23		
24		
25		
26		
27		
28		
29		
30		
31		
32		
33		
34		
35		
36		
37		
38		

MODE: ☐ Reading ●   ☐ Monologue ▲   ☑ Conversation ◆

Selection of Material to Elicit Baseline Samples

If clients can read, the reading selections should be varied from session to session and at a comfortable level so clients are interested in the material yet not struggling with the vocabulary. Popular library selections, basal readers, children's newspapers and magazines, or other similar material are appropriate for Level I. For secondary school age clients and adults, novels, news magazines, or newspaper articles can be used. Clients also may choose their own reading materials.

Topics of interest to the client should be used for the monologue as well; they should be varied from session to session. If clients prepare a monologue before the session, several valuable minutes of treatment time are saved. When young clients have difficulty continuing a monologue for two minutes without assistance, they can be helped by questions, such as "Who did that?" or "Why did you do that?" Suggested topics for monologues include:

- The plot of a book
- The plot of a TV show
- What happened at school or work that day
- What the client did over the weekend
- A favorite vacation site
- Description of a family member or friend
- Explanation of a hobby or video game
- How to construct an object, such as a model
- A current sports event (teams, play-offs)
- Stuttering problems and previous treatment activities
- Political issues or a specific politician
- Career goals or current occupation

Eye Contact

Stutterers often fail to make eye contact with others while engaging in conversation. This problem needs to be addressed directly. It should be brought to the client's attention along with other stuttering behaviors in the identification stage of this program. During subsequent monologue baselines at the beginning of each session, such clients should be reminded to look at the clinician while speaking. Saying "Look at me" and then smiling at clients as they glance quickly in the clinician's direction is one way to desensitize them. By the eighth or tenth session, the client should be able to look at the clinician while speaking for at least 30% of a monologue.

The Identification Stage

Goals of the identification stage of the program include defining the three major types of stuttering behaviors and any relevant secondary behaviors for the client. Then, the client must also practice identifying these behaviors in his own speech.

Defining Stuttering Behaviors

The clinician should begin teaching clients about disfluencies during the first or second treatment session because they must understand these behaviors thoroughly, a worthy long-range goal in itself. By understanding and predicting each type of disfluency that can occur, clients can select and use the appropriate technique to change the utterance to a fluent one and thus be in control.

The Three Types of Disfluencies

A simple way to introduce stuttering behavior is to tell the client three basic types of disfluencies that can occur:

- Repetitions
- Prolongations
- Blocks

Then, define and demonstrate each type. Once the client understands these definitions, they should be written on the first page of the speech book. From then on, the client becomes responsible for understanding and remembering them.

Repetition: Repeating a whole word, part of a word, or phrase or simply saying a word, part of a word, or a group of words over and over again. This type of disfluency also can be called *repeating*. Examples:

> *Whole Word Repetitions:* I can't can't can't come over today.
> *Part-Word Repetition:* I c-c-c-c-can't come over today.
> *Phrase Repetition:* I can't I can't I can't come over today.

Prolongation: Prolonging or extending a sound, usually on a vowel or fricative sounds, such as unvoiced [th], [f], [s], [sh], or their voiced cognates. These sounds are too long. Young children can remember this type of disfluency as *too long*. Examples:

- I waaaaaaaaant to go home.
- He ssssssaid I could.
- Sheeeeeeee won't let me do it.

Blocks: Usually occur on stop consonants or on vowels. A *block* can be defined for a young child as "getting ready to talk, and the word doesn't come out." Parents and adult clients can be given a more complex description, such as "cessation or stoppage of the airflow, either at the level of the vocal cords or at the place in the mouth where the consonant is made." These are only suggested definitions; the vocabulary of the explanation should be tailored to the cognitive level of the client. Demonstrations may include blocking on [b] with the lips, on [d] with the tongue tip pressed against the alveolar ridge, and on words beginning with vowels with the vocal folds adducted. Young children can remember this type of disfluency as *getting stuck*.

Secondary Behaviors

Explanations of *secondary behaviors* should be given to clients. Any starters or fillers in their speech, such as "uh uh uh" or "you know you know," are considered stutters. Clients can remember these as *extra words*. If a client exhibits secondary behaviors, such as eye blinks, head nods, nasal flares, or foot or finger tapping, these are considered additional types of stuttering behaviors.

Discussions of secondary behaviors should be brief to avoid making clients feel tense or upset. Aside from the importance of recognizing these behaviors as secondary to stuttering, identifying them also provides a form of desensitization for the client. Some clients never have had an opportunity to confront or discuss these somewhat unusual behaviors openly. If children show concern about these behaviors, they may be told such behaviors decrease as stuttering decreases.

Teaching Level I Clients to Identify Disfluencies

Once children understand the different types of disfluencies, the time has come to begin identifying their own disfluencies. When they are aware of disfluencies that can occur and can identify each type of stutter that may be exhibited, they are ready to select the appropriate fluency targets to overcome these stuttering behaviors.

To do this, particularly for the youngest clients, present two cups, one labeled "Mr. Yes" and the other "Mr. No," and a pile of poker chips, tokens, crayons, or other small safe objects (photocopy the drawings of the "Mr. Yes" and "Mr. No" clowns at the end of this book and attach them to the cups). Then, follow these steps to teach the client to identify disfluencies.

Step 1

Instruct the client as follows:

> "I will read aloud (or talk). Every time I stutter, let me get the whole word out, and then say 'Stop!' If you stop me after each time I stutter, you can feed Mr. Yes. If you let a stutter go by, you must feed Mr. No."

Then, talk or read aloud from high-interest material, stuttering frequently and demonstrating all the types of stutters. After the child says "Stop!" and "feeds" a cup with the selected item, ask what kind of stutter occurred to help the child use the appropriate terms.

Criterion: Proceed to Step 2 when the client can label the occurrence of disfluencies with 90% accuracy on twenty responses (18/20).

Step 2

Remove all the chips from the cups, and place them in front of the client. Say:

> "When I stutter this time, wait until I get the word out. Then, say 'Stop!' If you can tell me what kind of stutter it was, you can feed Mr. Yes. If you cannot, you must feed Mr. No. The three types of stuttering to remember are *repeating, too long,* and *getting stuck.*"

Listening in this way is a very unfamiliar skill. A child may require two sessions to understand the task and respond appropriately. These disfluencies can be made obvious, and some of the same starters or fillers the client exhibits may be presented.

Criterion: The client must have 75% correct on at least twenty trials (15/20) to go to Step 3.

Step 3

Remove all the chips from the cups, display them, and instruct the client as follows:

> "This time I want you to read (or tell me all about)_____.
> Every time you stutter, I will say 'Stop!' I must tell you what kind of stutter it was so I may feed Mr. Yes. Make sure I say the right kind."

Engage in this activity for five to eight minutes. Make some errors in judging the type of disfluency, and see if the client catches them.

Criterion: No criterion is necessary to complete Step 3; it is a relaxed playful phase of the identification process. The client may not stutter or may exhibit just a few disfluencies.

Step 4

Remove all the chips from the cups, and place them in front of the client. Instruct the child as follows:

> "Now I'd like you to talk to me. Every time you stutter, tell me what kind of stutter it was. If you are correct, you can feed Mr. Yes."

Criterion: The child must attain 60% accuracy on ten responses (6/10).

The client may not stutter a great deal during this activity, even though it is a difficult task. A reduction in disfluencies per minute on baseline charts during the identification phase also may occur. **Increasing the child's awareness of disfluencies usually reduces them initially, especially in young children.**

Teaching Level II Clients to Identify Disfluencies

Once the different types of disfluencies have been explained, clients are ready to begin the identification stage of the program. *Tell the client:* "Now we are ready to begin identification. As you read, I will interrupt you each time you stutter by saying 'there.' Please do not be offended; this is a learning experience to train you to identify your own disfluencies."

Step 1

As the client reads or (only if unable to read) talks, identify each disfluency visually and audibly. Say "there," click a hand counter, or use any other appropriate means to do so. Do this activity for five to eight minutes. Avoid prolonging this task because it may make the client very uncomfortable.

Step 2

Next, read or talk aloud for about five to eight minutes. Interject different kinds of disfluencies as you speak, allowing the client to identify *your* disfluencies and tell what kind of stuttering occurred after each instance. Doing this reinforces the client's new knowledge and understanding of the types of disfluencies.

Criterion: The client must have 80% correct on at least 20 trials (16/20) to go to Step 3.

Step 3

In this step the client reads or talks while you identify the disfluencies together. Ask the client to signal recognition of each disfluency by raising a finger, rather than speaking, to avoid interrupting fluency. Slightly delay saying "there" to let the client take the lead.

Criterion: None.

Step 4

The client continues reading and signaling his disfluencies while the clinician counts silently. When in agreement, you can say "good" or "right" quietly after each.

These steps can be completed in one session or repeated in the next if the client appears to need more clarification. The identification stage is usually enjoyable for clients because it provides so much information new to them. Although still not able to control disfluencies, the individual leaves this session with a positive attitude for the sessions to come.

Target Training

After the client reaches criterion on all tasks in the identification stage, target training begins. Target behaviors form a hierarchy of skills clients learn to incorporate into their speech repertoire. Fluent speakers use these techniques automatically. Stutterers must acquire them consciously and perfect each of the targets.

Target Definitions

This stage begins by giving clients the page of Target Definitions appropriate for their cognitive level (using a highlighter to introduce and emphasize each one is recommended). Then, the corresponding worksheets are used to practice and perfect each technique. These techniques should be reviewed frequently throughout this training because the skills build upon each other. Once a target is presented and highlighted, the client becomes responsible for knowing its meaning.

Stepping Up to Fluency 2
Target Definitions
Level I

Full Breath

Take in a deep breath every time you get ready to begin talking. Then, speak as soon as you start to breathe out.

Easy Onset

Use easy onset only for words beginning with vowel sounds. After you take a full breath, say the word in a very quiet voice, almost whispering. Then, get louder as you "go up the hill."

Continuous Speech

Connect words so no spaces are between them. Do not chop them up.

Light Contact

Use light contact for consonants, especially [p], [b], [t], [d], [k], and [g]. Say these sounds very gently and easily. Keep your lips, tongue, and jaw very loose.

Phrasing

Read or talk in units of no more than five or six words. Group words together by what they mean. Always stop at punctuation marks. Take a full breath before each phrase, and use easy onset or light contact to begin each phrase.

Stepping Up to Fluency 2
Target Definitions
Level II

Full Breath

Inhale enough air to sustain a complete phrase. Then, speak immediately upon exhalation.

Easy Onset

After taking a full breath, gently initiate the beginning sound, gradually increasing in loudness. Note: This target is used only for words beginning with vowel sounds.

Continuous Phonation or Continuous Speech

Move slowly between words without noticeable gaps. In other words, speak without choppiness, linking your words together.

Light Contact

Produce initial consonant sounds very lightly and easily with no tension in the articulators (tongue, lips, jaw, larynx, or voice box). Be sure to use light contact especially on plosive sounds, such as [p], [b], [t], [d], [k], and [g].

Phrasing

Read or talk in units of no more than seven or eight words; group words according to meaning and punctuation. Take a full breath before each phrase; use easy onset or light contact for the initial sound of the phrase.

Full Breath

Full breath is defined as taking in enough air to sustain a complete phrase, then speaking immediately upon exhalation. Full breath can be explained to younger clients as taking in a good deep breath so you have enough air to say a short sentence, then, talking right away as you breathe out.

Fluent speech requires prolonged, controlled exhalation that is different from the restful breathing used when not vocalizing. In contrast, many clients who stutter use *inefficient breathing patterns,* such as upper chest breathing or speaking on residual air.

To speak fluently, clients must learn to use efficient breathing patterns. After taking an adequate breath to abduct the vocal cords, they must speak immediately upon exhalation to avoid a hard glottal attack. Sufficient breath support is necessary to avoid speaking on residual air.

Defining and demonstrating *full breath* and *shallow breath* explain this target. The definition should be copied in the client's speech book. Clinicians may show clients approximately where the diaphragm is by moving their hands vertically, palm facing upward, down their own body as they inhale. Clients should be encouraged to try this several times, then move on to the second target, easy onset.

Easy Onset

Easy onset is the most important target of this stage of the program. Clients appreciate its usefulness as the hierarchy of their skills progresses. *Easy onset* is used to initiate speech only if the utterance begins with a vowel. Important: Once vocalization is begun, the client should never break phonation to use an easy onset for a vowel within a phrase.

For Level I clients, easy onset is defined as follows:

> *Easy onset is used only to say words that begin with vowel sounds. To use easy onset, take a full breath, then say the word in a very quiet voice, almost whispering. Then, get louder as you "go up the hill."*

This target should be described to the client and highlighted in the speech book. Then, the worksheet entitled "Easy Onset Words" is introduced.

For Level II clients, the definition is:

> *Easy Onset: After taking a full breath, gently initiate the sound, gradually increasing in loudness. This target is used for initial vowel words only.*

The diagram on the worksheet shows how to use the technique of *easy onset* to say the word "each." To **demonstrate**, the clinician can trace the line of the diagram with a finger while saying the word, first taking a *full breath*, then immediately upon exhalation beginning to phonate from a momentary whisper to a very quiet [i] or "e" sound, gradually increasing in loudness while following the curve of the diagram. When the top of the curve is reached (where the letters "ch" are printed), the voice should be approaching a normal conversational volume (approximately sixty decibels). The voice should not be stopped dramatically but faded slightly to the intersecting line as the curve indicates. This task is both auditory and visual; clients need the clinician's modeling to understand the target.

The words in this exercise roughly follow the familiar vowel trapezoid from high front vowels through low back vowels. This manner of presentation allows the client to *tune in* to each articulatory posture in conjunction with the *full breath* and increase in loudness for each word.

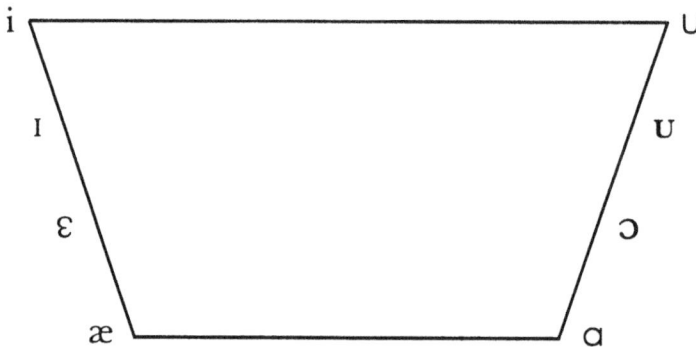

For this exercise, present the enlarged Easy Onset Curve facing toward the client. Each word on the list should be said slowly and deliberately by the clinician. Then, the client repeats each word while using a finger to trace the enlarged curve. The importance of taking a *full breath* before every word is stressed at this stage. A + or − should be marked after each stimulus item for visual feedback. This also helps identify any vowel sounds that give the client special difficulty.

A stopwatch should also be used during this exercise. To demonstrate the slow, deliberate production of the *easy onset*, the clinician takes a full breath, then clicks on the stopwatch while initiating voicing. The clinician continues to say the word and trace a finger along the curve for at least two and a half seconds. As the client says each word, the stopwatch is used in the same way with the time stated after each, saying, for example, "1.7 seconds too short" or "3.4 seconds too long."

As proficiency is gained, the client may use the smaller easy onset curve. For the words beginning with the "long" [u] sound or the letter "y," (the last 5 words on the list), the client is asked to pretend the initial vowel is "e" then "u," blending the two vowels together into a diphthong. This facilitates the necessary gradual increase in loudness, because saying the very quiet [e] sound is the easiest way to begin *easy onset* after taking a *full breath*. Level I clients may be asked to make a "smiley face" while saying [e], then blend it into a [u]. This can be called "making an ē face" for older clients.

Once this target is performed correctly, the client is fluent on all these words; if the airflow and voice onset are done properly, blocking is impossible. Persistence and repetition may be needed for the client to achieve total fluency; one to three sessions may be required to perfect this technique for saying single words. As the client gains proficiency at this target, *easy onset* should be practiced at a faster, more natural rate, and use of the stopwatch can be discontinued. At this point in treatment, a reinforcing activity can help keep many children motivated. A reinforcer that can be given quickly should be used so the young child does not lose concentration. Placing a sticker in the speech book after every five or eight responses works well, or the child might move a piece along a game board.

To proceed to the next level, the client must attain 100% accuracy at the more rapid rate without the clinician's model and without tracing the curve. For nonreaders to meet this criterion, the clinician says each word without using the fluency targets. The client responds, using *full breath* and *easy onset* on each word. At the end of the session, the Easy Onset Words worksheet should be placed in the speech book so the client can practice this target at home. Only those words the client can produce correctly without clinician model should be assigned for home practice.

Easy Onset Words: Level I and II

each	I
ears	I'm
east	on
even	or
eat	oh
easy	oak
in	own
inch	only
if	us
ill	under
inside	ugly
end	up
any	use
egg	yes
apple	yell
after	yellow
at	yesterday

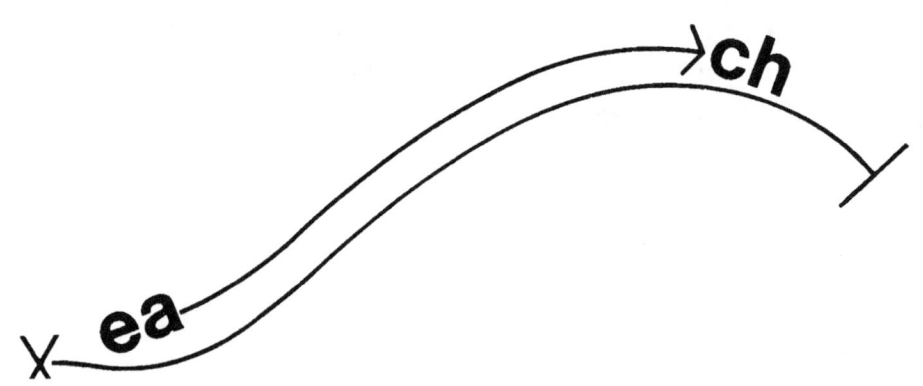

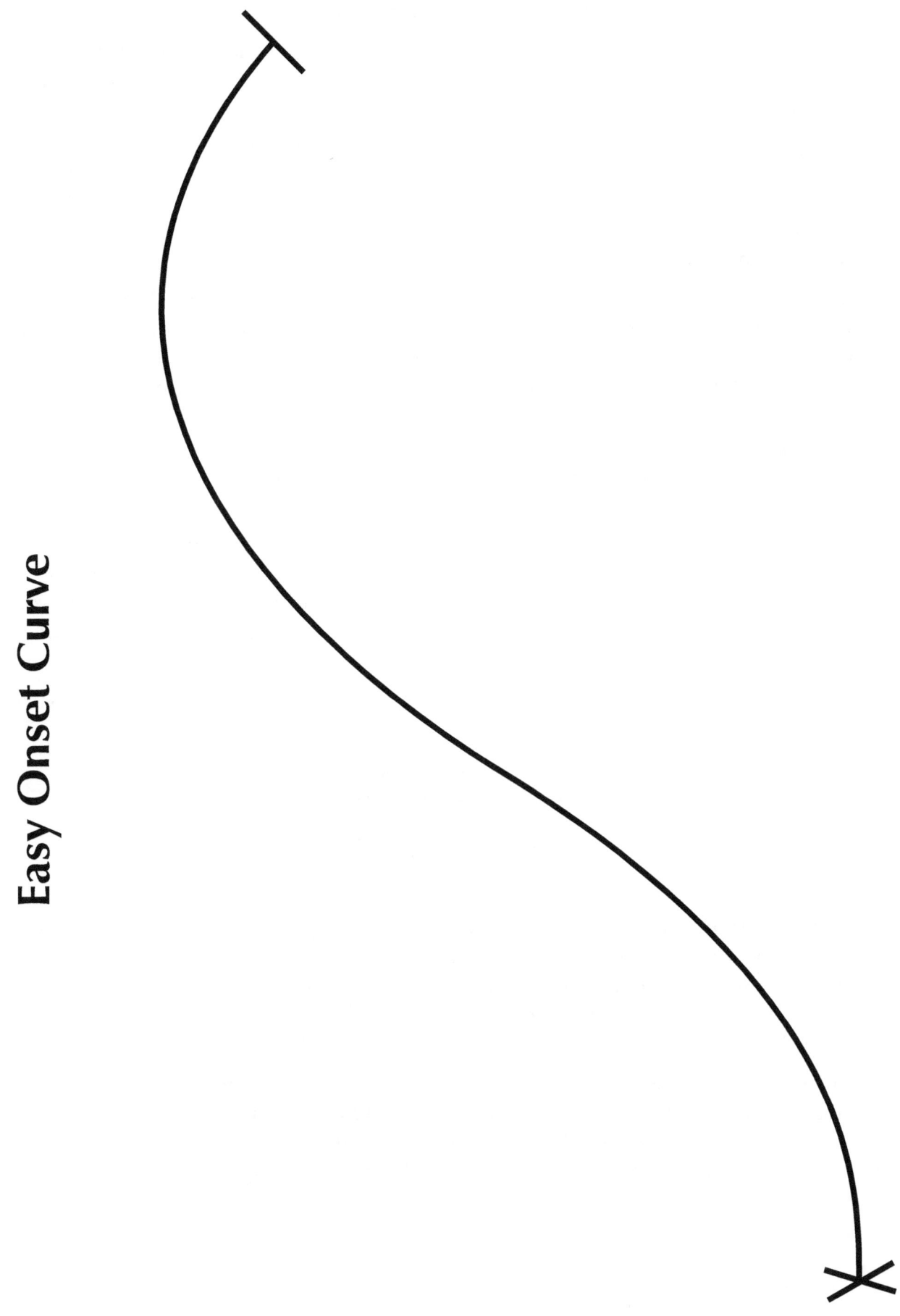

Continuous Speech

Once the client is proficient using *easy onset* in single words, training is begun for the third target of the program, *continuous speech*. *Continuous speech* can be explained to the Level I client in this way:

> *Connect your words so no spaces are between them. Do not chop them up.*

Level II clients can be instructed:

> *Move slowly between words without noticeable gaps. In other words, speak without choppiness. Link your words together.*

The worksheet of Easy Onset Phrases appropriate to the client's level should be used, then put in the speech book. The *continuous speech* technique should be demonstrated in combination with the techniques of *full breath* and *easy onset*. A hierarchy of techniques is now forming. The clinician demonstrates by reading each phrase, prolonging only the initial vowel sound and connecting the words and emphasizing the *full breath* and *easy onset* targets. Then, the client repeats each phrase. *Note:* These phrases contain the same words as the Easy Onset Words list. A quick review of that list may be necessary at this time.

If the client is breaking up phrases, this should be pointed out immediately and the error demonstrated. The client should be asked to place two or three fingertips lightly on the larynx while vocalizing the phrase to *feel* the continuous vibration. The voice box (larynx) can be compared to a car motor by explaining that once the "speech motor" is turned on, it should be kept "running."

No curve is to be used as a visual cue. However, the words can be connected with a pencil to give a visual cue. Example:

Clients must be reminded that only one easy onset is necessary per phrase because no break should occur between words if another word beginning with a vowel sound is found in that phrase. Initially, the targets are exaggerated; then, stress and intonation are changed once clients near criterion. This makes the phrases more meaningful and also helps them transfer this skill to conversational speech.

Adult stutterers who struggle with clonic blocks and use an extremely slow rate usually have difficulty varying their stress and intonation. They are so concerned with the *full breath*, *easy onset*, and *continuous speech* aspects that their production of the phrases may be monotonous, regardless of models provided by the clinician.

A fresh page of easy onset phrases is provided to the client with one word in each phrase highlighted as it is modeled by the clinician, then repeated by the client. Next, the clinician repeats the same phrase, highlighting and stressing a different word in the phrase while pointing out that changing the stress on one word can change the entire meaning of the phrase. For example, "*yesterday* it rained" has a different meaning from "yesterday it *rained*." After practicing one column of phrases this way, clients may want to try this on their own, even having the clinician guess which word is accented.

Clients remain at this level until their performance is 100% accurate on all phrases without a model. If a client is a nonreader, each phrase may be said in a normal voice; that is, without using any fluency targets. Then the client is asked to repeat the phrase using "all your targets." Again, speech will be fluent if the techniques are used correctly.

This is a very exciting time! Clinicians will be sure to show enthusiasm and offer lots of verbal praise. As in previous lessons, allowing younger clients to put stickers in the speech book or move a piece along a game board after every five or eight responses reinforces their success.

While working on the Easy Onset Phrases, the vocabulary acquired to date should be reviewed. Clients can answer questions about the three types of disfluencies, name the targets learned thus far, and explain the targets in their own words. Even children in the primary grades are able to do this. Once a client can explain the types of stuttering and name the targets, one foot is on the first step toward fluency.

Questions to Elicit Easy Onset Phrases

An enjoyable way to practice Easy Onset Phrases after the criterion has been reached is to ask questions clients can answer using the printed phrase. A list of Sample Questions to Elicit Easy Onset Phrases is provided. For example, if asked "Which dog gets a bone?" the client can reply "each one," or ask "Where is the turtle?" to elicit the response "in the yard," continuing down the list in this manner. Stating the number of each question helps the client find the corresponding answer. This facilitates more informal interaction between client and clinician along with the functional use of targets, even this early in the program. Sample questions provided can be used, or names and personal references can be added to the questions to personalize them for individual clients. Emphasize that this is a *practice* activity and clients are to respond with the printed phrase rather than inventing an original response. The questions have several possible answers; in some cases, the target phrase is not necessarily the most natural answer.

If necessary, the client should be reminded to use the targets while enjoying this activity. If the client cannot read or recall the phrase, the question can be asked and then the response whispered. The client can then repeat the answer, using the targets. The Easy Onset Phrases can be assigned as home practice as soon as the client can do them correctly. Parents can use the Sample Questions to Elicit Easy Onset Phrases during home practice.

Easy Onset Sentences

Next, the Easy Onset Sentences worksheet appropriate to the client's level is introduced. Remind the client that *full breath, easy onset,* and *continuous speech* are to be used. The procedure is the same as that used for the phrases, having the client practice all sentences dependently and independently of clinician's model.

Five phrases and six sentences beginning with "I" are included for Level I clients because children in the primary grades usually begin their utterances this way. One phrase and one sentence require the child's name, which is important because stutterers often experience blocks when saying their own names. This exercise helps clients try the *full breath* and *easy onset* targets as strategies to master this obstacle.

Because the client's goal is to incorporate these techniques into everyday speech, natural stress and intonation are to be used saying these sentences. Highlighting and stressing different words enables adult stutterers to learn to vary their stress and intonation. Asking the Sample Questions to Elicit Easy Onset Sentences or, as with the easy onset phrases, making up more personalized questions helps them use the targets in conversation. If the client is a nonreader, using the approach outlined for the Easy Onset Phrases is also suitable for the Easy Onset Sentences.

If the client cannot maintain *continuous speech* through the easy onset sentences after several trials using this worksheet, it should be put aside and training begun on the next target. Reinforcing the habit of breaking *continuous speech* within a sentence must be avoided. Later in the program, the Practice Pages 1-4 worksheets will give the client further practice increasing the length of utterances. A review of easy onset sentences at that time is appropriate.

Easy Onset Phrases: *Level I*

1. each one
2. ears are big
3. east and west
4. even me
5. Easter eggs
6. eat your lunch
7. easy work
8. I want more
9. in the yard
10. inch long
11. if I can
12. ill at school
13. inside the house
14. I am home
15. end of day
16. any cookies?
17. eggs are good
18. apple trees
19. at the pool
20. after we go
21. I see you
22. I am hungry
23. on the bed
24. oh I forgot
25. oak trees grew
26. own a doll
27. only she will
28. I am _____ .*(client's name)*
29. under the chair
30. ugly old dog
31. up the wall
32. use it all
33. yes, I will
34. yell at him
35. yellow shirt
36. yesterday it rained

Sample Questions to Elicit Easy Onset Phrases: *Level I*

1. Which dog gets a bone?
2. What are the clown's ears like?
3. Which way does this road go?
4. Who is hungry?
5. What's in your basket?
6. What should I do now?
7. What did you do in school after lunch?
8. What do you want?
9. Where is the turtle?
10. How long is a green bean?
11. Will you come over to my house?
12. How were you this morning?
13. Where is your dad?
14. Where are you now?
15. When do you rest?
16. What did you ask your mom?
17. What's good for breakfast?
18. What can grow on a farm?
19. Where is your brother?
20. Should we watch TV now or later?
21. Who do you see?
22. How do you feel?
23. Where is the doll? (or robot or other toy)
24. Did you bring your pictures?
25. What grew in your yard?
26. What do you own? (or what do your sisters own)
27. Who will help you with your homework?
28. Who are you?
29. Where is the kitten?
30. What do I hear barking?
31. Where did the spider crawl?
32. May I use some of the milk?
33. Will you color this picture?
34. What can I do to quiet the dog?
35. What will you wear to my party?
36. How was the weather yesterday?

Stepping Up to Fluency 2. Copyright © 2017 by Janice Pechter Ellis. This page may be reproduced for individual instructional use only.

Easy Onset Sentences: *Level I*

1. Each one is ready for school.
2. Ears are on your head.
3. East and west are on a map.
4. Even he can do it.
5. Easter eggs are many colors.
6. Eat your soup slowly.
7. Easy work is fun to do.
8. I want more fruit.
9. In the yard is a frog.
10. Inches are on a ruler.
11. If you go, I'll go too.
12. I'll tell you a secret.
13. Inside the room is my cat.
14. I am not sleepy now.
15. End of the movie is good.
16. Any more cookies for me?
17. Eggs are good to eat.
18. Apples are very sweet.
19. And I went to bed.
20. At the pool is my mom.
21. After we play, I'll go home.
22. I'll see you later.
23. I am reading a storybook.
24. On the bed is my puppy.
25. Oh, I need to go home.
26. Only you know my name.
27. I am_____. *(client's name)*
28. Ugly old dogs were barking.
29. Using the crayons is fun.
30. Yes, I will come to your party.
31. Yelling can wake you up.
32. Yellow is a nice color.
33. Yesterday was her birthday.

Stepping Up to Fluency 2. Copyright © 2017 by Janice Pechter Ellis. This page may be reproduced for individual instructional use only.

Sample Questions to Elicit Easy Onset Sentences: *Level I*

1. Who is ready for school?
2. What is on my head? *(putting your hands up toward ears)*
3. What can you see on a map?
4. Who can do this trick?
5. What colors are Easter eggs?
6. Should I gobble up my soup?
7. How do you like easy work?
8. What do you want to eat?
9. What is in the yard?
10. What can you see on a ruler?
11. Should we go to the store?
12. What will you whisper to me?
13. Where is your cat?
14. Are you ready for bed?
15. Do you like the movie Frozen? *(or any other movie)*
16. What did you ask me?
17. What do you like for breakfast?
18. What do apples taste like?
19. And what happened after you brushed your teeth?
20. Who is at the swimming pool?
21. When will you go home?
22. Goodbye,_____ . *(client's name)*
23. What are you reading?
24. Where is your puppy?
25. Where are you going?
26. Who knows your name?
27. Please tell me your full name?
28. Which dogs were barking?
29. Do you like coloring?
30. Will you come to my party?
31. What happens when people yell?
32. What is one nice color?
33. When was your teacher's birthday?

Stepping Up to Fluency 2. Copyright © 2017 by Janice Pechter Ellis. This page may be reproduced for individual instructional use only.

Easy Onset Phrases: *Level II*

1. each one
2. ears can hear
3. even me
4. eat your lunch
5. easy lessons
6. Easter vacation
7. in the house
8. inch by inch
9. ill at ease
10. if I can
11. inside the house
12. anyone here?
13. end of the day
14. ever go home?
15. eggs are good
16. apple pies
17. and I will
18. after I go
19. at the lake
20. I am _____ .*(client's name)*
21. I'm not ready yet
22. on the table
23. or I won't
24. over the hill
25. oh, I forgot
26. oak trees grew
27. own a house
28. only he will
29. under the tree
30. ugly old rug
31. up the wall
32. use it all
33. usually I will
34. yet she came
35. yesterday it rained
36. yes, I do

Sample Questions to Elicit Easy Onset Phrases: *Level II*

1. Which dog is outside?
2. What can ears do?
3. Who is hungry?
4. What should I do at noon?
5. Do you like easy lessons or hard ones?
6. When will you visit?
7. Where is your Dad?
8. How does a worm move?
9. How do you feel before a test *or* at the doctor's office? *(ask just one)*
10. Will you come over today?
11. Where is the cat?
12. What did you say when you entered the house?
13. When do you relax?
14. *- no question -*
15. What is good for breakfast?
16. What did your mother/father/spouse bake?
17. Bob will help, and who else?
18. When will you call me?
19. Where is the boathouse?
20. Who are you?
21. Are you ready to go?
22. Where is the gift?
23. *- no question -*
24. Where is the barn?
25. Why didn't you come to speech yesterday? *or* Did you call your friend?
26. What kind of trees grew?
27. What would you like to own?
28. Who will help you?
29. Where is the rock?
30. What is by the back door?
31. Where did the monkey climb?
32. Should I use all of it, or just part?
33. Will you enjoy the concert?
34. I thought your mother didn't like rock music.
35. How was the weather yesterday?
36. Do you enjoy swimming (diving, skiing, etc.)?

Easy Onset Sentences: *Level II*

1. Each student came inside.
2. Ears are for hearing.
3. Even I can do it.
4. Eat your lunch slowly.
5. Easy work is boring.
6. Easter vacation was nice.
7. In the room is a chair.
8. Inches and feet are measurements.
9. Ill children stay at home.
10. If you tell me, I'll know.
11. Inside the yard is a garden.
12. Anyone knows the answer.
13. End of the movie is sad.
14. Every picture tells a story.
15. Eggs and bacon taste good.
16. Apple pastry is better hot.
17. And then he left.
18. After a while the rain stopped.
19. At my house is a man.
20. I am _____. *(client's full name)*
21. I'm afraid of snakes.
22. On the shelf is my folder.
23. Over my head is a cloud.
24. Oh, I forgot to come.
25. Oak trees grew outside.
26. Owning a house is my dream.
27. Only he knows the answer.
28. Under the bridge is a road.
29. Unhappy people left early.
30. Up the stairs is my bedroom.
31. Use it wisely and it will last.
32. Yes, she knew I would go.
33. Yelling is very loud.
34. Yellow is not my favorite color.

Sample Questions to Elicit Easy Onset Sentences: *Level II*

1. Where are the students?
2. What are your ears for?
3. Who can do this exercise?
4. Should I eat in a hurry?
5. Do you enjoy easy work?
6. How was your vacation?
7. What furniture is in the room?
8. What are two common measurements?
9. What do ill children do?
10. How will you know the answer?
11. What is inside the yard?
12. Who knows the answer?
13. How is the end of the movie "The Lion King"/ "The Notebook"? *(or other movie)*
14. What do pictures tell us?
15. What tastes good for breakfast?
16. Do you like the pastry hot or cold?
17. What did he do after lunch?
18. Was it still raining?
19. Who is at your house?
20. What is your name?
21. Do you like reptiles?
22. Where is your speech folder?
23. Where is the cloud?
24. Where were you yesterday at 1:30?
25. What kind of trees grew outside?
26. What is your lifelong dream?
27. Does anyone know the answer?
28. Where is a road?
29. Who left the party early?
30. Where is your bedroom?
31. How can I make this glue last?
32. Did your mother know that you'd go?
33. Which is louder — singing or yelling?
34. Would you like to paint the room yellow?

Light Contact

The fourth target, *light contact*, is defined for Level I clients as follows:

> Use this target only with consonants, especially [p], [b], [t], [d], [k], and [g]. Say these sounds very gently and easily. Keep your lips, tongue, and jaw very loose. Making these sounds too tightly might cause you to get stuck.

Then, *hard* contacts on *boy, girl*, and *puppy* are demonstrated to illustrate this point.

For Level II clients, *light contact* is defined as follows:

> Produce the initial consonant sounds very lightly and easily, with no tension in the articulators (tongue, lips, jaw, larynx, or voice box), specifically for plosive sounds [p], [b], [t], [d], [k], and [g].

Tension is explained by comparing it to how a tightly clenched fist feels. Saying words such as *boy, table,* and *deep* with tight, hard contacts show how this is done with the articulators.

The Speech Helpers (Articulators)

At this point the client is introduced to the articulators (or "speech helpers," depending on the client's level). Speech helpers are *parts of the body that help people talk*. This concept is presented in the same manner it is explained to an articulation client. Reproducible line drawings are included to use as a visual guide and insert in the speech book. The client should look in a mirror throughout these exercises. The articulators are described in order from the front to the back of the mouth. After each has been discussed and understood, the client is asked, "What comes next?" Younger clients may color each diagram for positive reinforcement. Below are sample conversations for each diagram.

Lips: While looking in a mirror, the clinician asks the client to name the first thing seen on the face that helps with talking. If a client says "mouth," saying, "Yes, but what part of the mouth do you see first?" encourages the response "lips." Then, the clinician asks what sounds are made with lips ([b], [p], [m], [w]), instructing the client to watch in the mirror throughout the exercise. If necessary, instructing younger children to say, *Bob, pop, mom,* and *wow* cues these sounds. An association can be made by writing the letters for these four consonants next to the drawing of the lips.

Teeth: The clinician asks "What sounds do you make with your teeth?" ([f], [v], voiced and unvoiced [th]). "Try saying, *fat, valentine, thank you*. Look in the mirror as you say these words." Writing the letters for these sounds next to the teeth provides reinforcement.

Tongue: When the client guesses "tongue," the clinician points out the tongue has two parts, the tip and the back, then asks "What sounds do you make with the tongue tip? Repeat these sounds (not the letter names): [t], [d], [s], [z], [n], [l] and say the words *no, lady,* and *toe* to feel the contact. Now, what sounds do you make with your tongue pulled back? Try saying the sounds [k] and [g]." The association is made by writing the corresponding letters next to the tongue.

Alveolar Ridge or "Bumpy Part": Clients may say "gums" but probably will not guess "alveolar ridge." The clinician can ask, "What sounds do you make with your tongue touching the bumpy part of your mouth? Your tongue tip goes here to make the sounds [t], [d], [s], [z], [l], and [n]. Repeat these sounds after me." Writing the corresponding letters next to the illustration of the alveolar ridge reinforces this association.

Larynx or "Voice Box": The clinician asks, "Do you know which sounds you make with your vocal cords? *All the voiced sounds.* Feel your voice box, and repeat these sounds after me. Try to feel the vibration." The clinician should model all the long vowels and the consonant sounds [m], [n], [v], [d], and [z], then write the corresponding letters next to the illustration of the larynx.

This exercise in oral awareness is crucial for the client to understand and internalize the *light contact* target. Most clients, both young and old, are quite interested in this activity which should be presented as a discovery exercise. Clients should go over this exercise several times during the session for complete understanding. An effective homework assignment is for the client to show and explain the activities in this worksheet to a parent or significant other.

The Speech Helpers (Articulators)

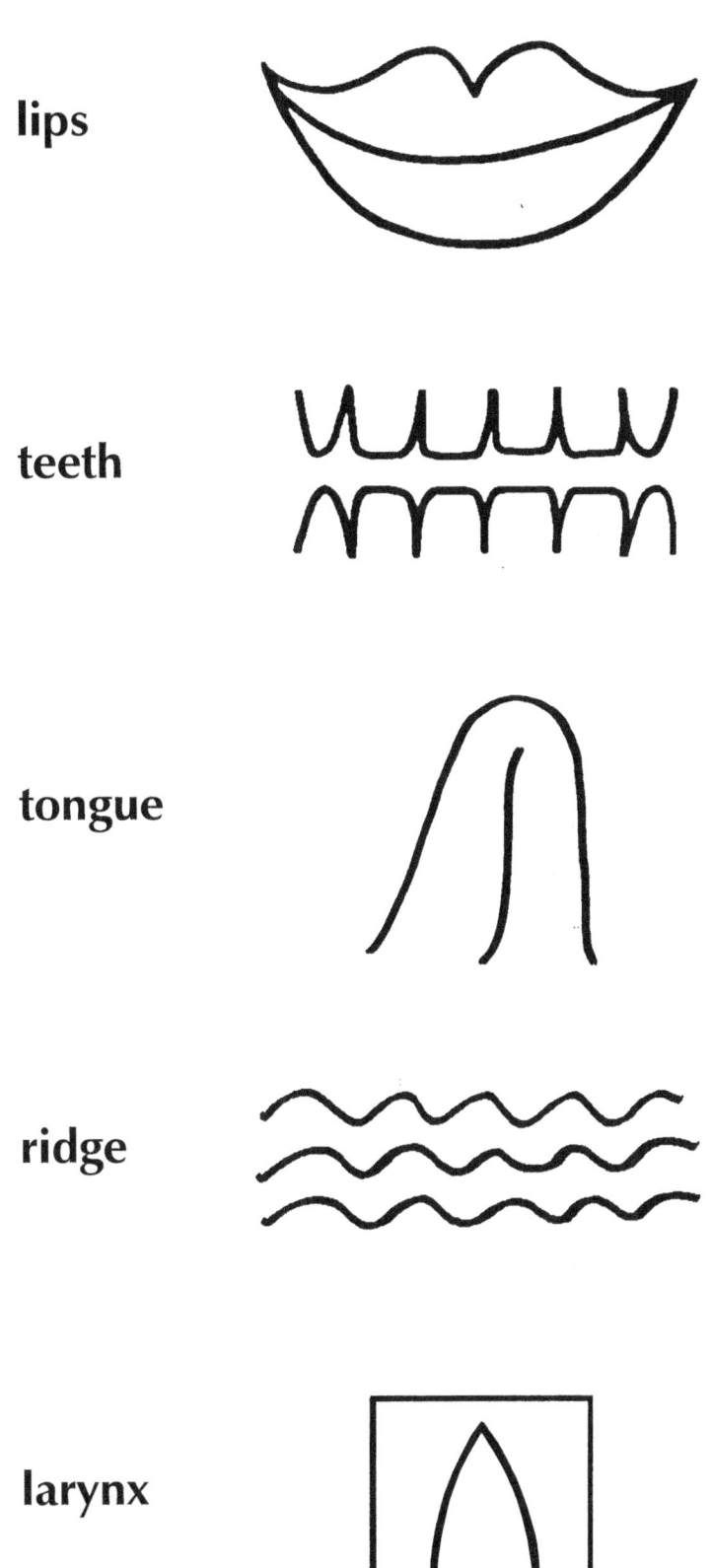

lips

teeth

tongue

ridge

larynx

Light Contact Word Lists

After the articulators are explained, the worksheets of *light contact* words beginning with [p] and [b] sounds are introduced. These are appropriate sounds with which to start training light contacts because feeling the direct contrast between hard contact and light contact is easy. When made with light contact, [p] sounds should sound almost like an [h], and the approximation of the lips should be only slightly audible. How to do this target incorrectly, making a very hard articulatory contact for the [p], should also be demonstrated and how this hard contact could become a block or a part-word repetition explained.

The client repeats each word in the list after the clinician models correct production. Feedback is provided for the client by marking a + or — after each word attempted (in the same way as for the easy onset target lists). Then, the word lists for the other stop sounds are presented, demonstrating hard contact on several words to show incorrect production.

When introducing each additional consonant sound, which speech helpers are involved in its production and whether the sound is voiced or unvoiced should be discussed. When producing words with the [k] and [g] sounds, the approximation of the tongue back to the soft palate is only slightly audible.

Discretion should be used regarding how many of these lists to practice in one session, with consideration given to the client's attention span and the time available Typically, at least two lists (one cognate pair) can be completed per session. Younger clients may need the reinforcement of moving a piece along a game board or putting stickers in their speech books after every eight correct responses.

Another activity to reinforce the learning of these targets is placing a sheet of paper over each page of *light contact* words so only two words are exposed at a time (such as "key" and "girl" on the [k] and [g] page). The client is asked to read each set of words, using both *light contact* and *continuous speech* and varying stress and intonation as the words are read. The word pairs can be read either from left to right or right to left; some of the combinations are humorous, making this an enjoyable activity.

Light Contact Picture Cards: Level I

Because many Level I clients are nonreaders or beginning readers, pictures can be used to supplement the word lists. Twelve reproducible pictures are included at the back of this book for each of the six consonant sounds; they may be photocopied as often as necessary and used as flash cards.

Using pictures has many advantages. Pictures can add interest and variety to the task of practicing. They may be taken home in the speech book to practice. The pictures for each sound can be presented after the corresponding word list; they may be used in cognate pairs or mixed together for review. Using picture cards enables clients to say each word independently of the clinician's model to reach the 100% mastery criterion. Clients can also make up phrases for these pictured words.

Light Contact Words

[p]	[b]
pan	beans
pot	beef
park	bank
pop	ball
pin	bath
pull	bacon
paint	bear
potato	bee
party	bus
puppy	book
peach	boy
peanuts	barking
pen	baby
pencil	bat
pets	barn
pour	butter
picture	boat
pie	bake
pine	banana
pole	bunk
pear	bed
pain	bells
poor	box
pudding	band

Light Contact Words

[t]	[d]
tea	deer
top	duck
tail	dog
table	dad
talk	dance
tall	dish
tears	dark
teach	doctor
team	doll
teeth	day
teacher	dime
tent	dirt
time	dozen
test	deep
tie	desk
tire	dots
toys	door
toad	donkey
towel	doughnut
tape	dove
toes	drink
tube	dress
tack	daisy
tiny	drum

Light Contact Words

[k]	[g]
key	girl
cat	gum
king	give
cap	goat
kitten	goose
cage	gas
call	gate
can	gull
car	game
cow	globe
cook	gift
corn	goodbye
cave	ghost
cowboy	golf
comb	garbage
carrots	gallon
kite	guitar
candy	gallop
canoe	gloves
candle	glass
coins	grapes
calf	grandfather
cane	gorilla
kiss	goal post

Strategies for Sounds Other than Plosives

This program requires practice on plosive sounds to train correct use of light contact. However, if a specific problem saying another sound, such as [l], [f], or voiced [th], is identified, a list of words containing these sounds should be prepared for practice. Any articulation list of age-appropriate words or picture stimulus cards containing the problem sound(s) will suffice. Which Speech Helpers are involved and how the *light contact* should be made should be discussed before the words are attempted; this gives clients strategies in advance for producing the different sounds fluently.

If [h] or [w] sounds are difficult, they may be demonstrated by showing how a *full breath* and awareness of rounded lips for the [w] sound will facilitate the next sound. The client rarely needs to practice lists of words for these sounds.

Because [s] and [sh] sounds are made by constricting, not stopping, the airway, a *light contact* cannot be used to produce these sounds. If [s] and [sh] are a problem, clients can be advised to "Make the sound, get off it right away, then go on to the next sound. Do not hold onto it." Any word lists or pictures available for these sounds are suitable for practicing this strategy.

To review, the client should be asked to name and discuss the targets learned so far.

Multisyllabic Words: *Level II*

Stutterers commonly have difficulty saying multisyllabic words. Quite often, a teenager or adult will substitute a shorter, simpler word for a desired word containing three or more syllables because the substitute word is easier to say than the multisyllabic word. Examples include using the word "large" for "astronomical" or "fun" for "delightful." This use of *circumlocution* hinders the person's communicative intent because the speaker's true meaning has not been conveyed.

The list of multisyllabic words can be presented to clients approximately fifteen years and older. To practice, they repeat each word after listening to the clinician's model, tapping out the syllables on fingers as the words are spoken, and using a different finger for each beat. They then immediately tell how many syllables were felt. Counting the syllables as the client carefully articulates the word provides valuable auditory and tactile feedback on each word. After reaching 100% accuracy on the syllable count and pronunciation of all the words, the client says the words independently, without actually using fingers to count the syllables, but tapping the fingers on a table (or lap, if necessary) to help maintain a steady pace through multisyllabic words in a conversation.

Multisyllabic Words

communicate	binoculars
dictionary	experiment
culinary	segregation
economics	terminal
delightful	practical
inhibition	application
traditional	representation
decoration	satisfaction
habitual	predictable
conversational	latitude
relaxation	atmosphere
longitude	metamorphic
photographic	procrastination
demographic	preparation
disappointment	embarrassed
personal	watermelon
intermediate	scholarship
presidential	population
personality	intentionally
consideration	hippopotamus
obligation	equilibrium
festival	biological
automobile	astronomical
hypochondriac	dictatorship
autobiography	nonjudgmental
unforgettable	undisciplined
entertainment	perpendicular
instantaneous	underestimated

Practice Pages

After learning four of the five targets, the client is ready to begin the core drill of this program: *Practicing the targets using the worksheets that consist of words and phrases grouped in sets of ten for the client to read or recite.* These practice pages provide the opportunity to use the targets while saying frequently used words and phrases of increasing length. While practicing these lists, the client must decide which targets are suitable for each word or phrase. For example, words beginning with vowel sounds require *easy onset*; words with certain consonant sounds require *light contact,* regardless of the position of the consonant sound within the phrase. Clients must remember to take a *full breath* before every utterance and use *continuous speech* between words. Practice worksheets are provided for both Levels I and II.

Using the Practice Worksheets

In-Session Practice

This sequence of three steps should be followed for each page of practice materials:

1. For each list of ten, the clinician reads a word or phrase to model the targets, then the client repeats it.

2. The client reads all ten items in the same list without a model while the clinician keeps score. These first two steps are continued with each set of ten words until the client has read the entire practice page in order by groups, both with and without clinician model.

3. The client chooses any three groups of ten words or phrases from the practice page and reads them without a model. If all three lists are read using all relevant fluency targets with 100% accuracy, the client proceeds to the next practice page.

The last two steps can be accomplished with nonreaders or poor readers by:

- Saying each word or phrase without using any fluency targets, then instructing the client to say the stimulus item using "all your targets," or —

- Whispering the phrase and asking the client to repeat it, using the appropriate targets.

Many of the groupings are situational. This helps nonreaders anticipate, and possibly remember, these phrases after several repetitions.

This practice is redundant for the client, but the proficiency gained is well worth it. The words and phrases on the practice pages are common expressions for primary school children, so these drills prepare the client for carryover. Many of the phrases on Practice Pages 3 and 4 of Level I begin with "I". This is intentional, as young children do speak this way. Further improvement should be seen on the baseline charts as clients develop these skills.

Home Practice

Home practice is a crucial part of this program and necessary for success. The client should practice at home any worksheet completed with 100% accuracy in the treatment session. This involves scoring and practicing the exercises with interested family members. If the family is supportive, the client progresses more steadily.

Practice Pages

Practice Page 1

The words and phrases increase in complexity in the lists. Each list starts with words that begin with vowel sounds and [h], [m], [w], and voiced [th] – then progresses to plosives, sibilants, and consonant blends. Strategies for producing the plosive sounds have already been covered on the light contact worksheets. The client should be reminded to use the appropriate targets before progressing through the three steps.

Practice Page 2

Clients should be asked what target techniques they plan to use on this worksheet and be reminded to use *continuous speech* because this worksheet contains two words presented together. Progress through this practice page should take place in the same manner as Practice Page 1.

Practice Pages 3 and 4

Full breath is the important target to be emphasized here because breath must be adequate to support speech through these longer phrases. Practice Pages 3 and 4 may be utilized for several sessions, depending on the client's ability to incorporate all the targets learned to this point.

Supplemental Practice Pages 3 and 4

These worksheets are provided for Level II clients to use if the client has scores such as 100% - 100% - 90% or 100% - 80% - 100% for several sessions and is becoming frustrated trying to obtain three consecutive perfect scores on the same lists. The supplemental lists are also helpful for review later in the program.

Multisyllabic Words in Short Sentences

Level II clients are now ready to say multisyllabic words in short sentences, using the four techniques practiced so far – *full breath, easy onset, continuous speech,* and *light contact.* They may be reminded to tap fingers lightly when necessary to feel the different syllables in the italicized words. The client must be 100% accurate independently of clinician model to move on to the next unit of this program.

The Score Sheet

The reproducible score sheet can be used to monitor progress on the Practice Pages. Several blank copies should be provided for the client to keep in the speech book for recording home practice.

Scoring Instructions: Whenever the client fails to use a necessary target, the score drops 10%. For example, if the client forgets to use *full breath* twice and *light contact* once, the score is 70% for that list of ten words or phrases. The client is asked how many targets were missed after reading each list of ten to encourage self-recognition of errors. An ample number of score sheets should be provided because reaching the criterion for any given level may take several lines or even most of one entire score sheet.

To meet the criterion to advance to the next level, the client must perform the third step – any three lists recited without a model with 100% accuracy. When the client attains perfect accuracy on three consecutive lists of ten, the scores on the score sheet are circled to highlight this achievement. If the score is less than 100% on one of the three trials, the client should continue practicing the current worksheet until the criterion is met. On Practice Pages 2, 3, and 4, if clients score less than 100% on two out of three lists, they are to go back to the preceding practice page because they are not using one or more of the targets for fluent speech.

Stepping Up to Fluency 2: Score Sheet

Name _____

Criterion: To move ahead to the next practice page, the client must use all relevant fluency targets with 100% accuracy on three consecutive lists read *independently* of the clinician's model. If the client's score is less than 100% on one of the three lists (100%, 100%, 90%, for example), repeat the level. If the client's score is less than 100% on two out of three lists on Pages 2, 3, or 4 (such as 90%, 90%, 100%), return to the preceding level.

Date	Page	Scores		
_____	_____	_____	_____	_____
_____	_____	_____	_____	_____
_____	_____	_____	_____	_____
_____	_____	_____	_____	_____
_____	_____	_____	_____	_____
_____	_____	_____	_____	_____
_____	_____	_____	_____	_____
_____	_____	_____	_____	_____
_____	_____	_____	_____	_____
_____	_____	_____	_____	_____
_____	_____	_____	_____	_____
_____	_____	_____	_____	_____
_____	_____	_____	_____	_____
_____	_____	_____	_____	_____
_____	_____	_____	_____	_____

Stepping Up to Fluency 2. Copyright © 2017 by Janice Pechter Ellis. This page may be reproduced for individual instructional use only.

Practice Page 1: *Level I*

I	talk	mother
am	nice	white
how	ears	turkey
in	king	move
man	egg	window
why	four	teacher
house	cat	sentence
and	horse	homework
the	yes	cookies
no	eyes	pool
more	here	truck
it	pants	school
have	cows	table
walk	snow	puppy
this	dad	TV
she	tie	dinner
leg	pear	safety
he	seed	road
meat	care	looking
out	shoe	money
put	dog	Christmas
my	we	garden
home	black	silver
can	key	pencil
eat	stay	inside
say	blue	Easter
hair	into	peanuts
mice	lunch	garbage
red	carry	cowboy
sock	box	kitten

Stepping Up to Fluency 2. Copyright © 2017 by Janice Pechter Ellis. This page may be reproduced for individual instructional use only.

Practice Page 2: *Level I*

I am	go away
he is	in school
why not?	go home
easy lesson	see mother
who knows?	all done
come here	sister fell
on table	watch TV
ears hear	get dressed
eat lunch	you can
your seat	he cried
my eyes	where's Mom?
her hands	he's good
sit down	my book
over here	I'm sleepy
I saw	your bedtime
you know	my watch
he can	in class
she said	new book
two minutes	say that
can you?	don't touch
my bike	brother's car
your bat	fall down
hands off	catch me
dogs run	will you?
did he?	I'm late
eat candy	get mad
play ball	big girl
I forgot	white shirt
come in	funny clown
use it	use these

Practice Page 3: *Level I*

a big boy
my new game
I know you
come over here
my white cat
I want that
a pretty girl
where am I?
can I go?
she is here

he is late
should I start?
sit down now
use my pencil
I had milk
want some cookies?
I like that
we went home
that's my friend
what's her name?

he's too rough
I can't play
she fell down
are you hurt?
let's go home
where is daddy?
I know that
let's have fun
I saw you
in the park

my best friend
a yellow pencil
will you tell?
that is mine
open the door
come in please
where are you?
who is that?
that's my dad
he is tall

I am_____. *(name of client)*
he's a boy
she's a girl
he said no
Mom came home
where was she?
this is new
where's my lunch?
can I eat?
I want more

she's my teacher
here's my room
we are early
here's my desk
I have paper
a blue pen
three big crayons
did you see?
I like school
we play outside

Practice Page 4: *Level I*

here is my house
can we go in?
say hi to mom
this is my book
I like to read
he is my friend
I know that boy
please don't do that
I'm finished with that
my name is _____.

I like red best
let's go in here
can I play now?
I know that girl
she's in my class
what time is it?
can we watch that?
what's on TV now?
I like that show
we always do that

can I come in?
where is your mom?
I like that song
where is the puppy?
his name is Spot
he is so cute
I am hot now
can we wear shorts?
it's time for lunch
where is the car?

I like to swim
here is the pool
can we go in?
the water is cold
I broke my crayon
can I get more?
this is too big
I need the bathroom
where is the dog?
he is going outside

can we stay home?
I am too tired
this is really fun
who is your cousin?
the glass is broken
it's on the floor
can you fix it?
I'm sorry about that
can we go now?
I need to leave

when is your birthday?
I will be six
I want a rabbit
it's warm and soft
don't walk so fast
where is my dad?
I need a tissue
we forgot to go
is it too late?
we'll have a party

Practice Page 1: *Level II*

on	maybe	father
am	boat	person
is	did	nobody
and	when	together
the	end	someone
a	have	chimney
that	day	chair
he	two	place
to	edge	turkey
not	cry	hostess
there	stand	school
it	away	cave
I	nothing	climb
she	fall	sentence
they	cut	question
in	would	suit
man	where	pocket
lock	off	knife
go	will	window
went	cloud	sister
that	snow	books
out	love	ring
him	play	outfit
boy	feet	pencil
cause	rope	straight
mouse	into	speak
girl	garden	because
had	stone	anything
think	left	magazine
wife	type	since

Practice Page 2: *Level II*

I know	how come?
you are	new ring
they said	yellow pencil
in oven	brick wall
on table	close windows
he can	new outfit
we went	his bicycle
down there	mother's cat
up north	crayon box
early day	sister's dress
what time?	run away
could you?	new neighbors
who said?	big house
sit down	my address
down town	Christmas Day
in office	next week
use blue	her present
new shirt	bright client
dirty room	easy lesson
my nose	never forget
their horse	when's dinner?
at camp	why not?
my car	don't yell
why not?	name one
since when?	three years
book cover	ate lunch
eat dinner	first class
for father	what color?
not ready	old person
ten minutes	bring erasers

Practice Page 3: *Level II*

leave me alone
what's your name?
why is that?
she took it
Mom came home
when is breakfast?
a turkey cooking
potatoes with gravy
gum is sticky
green is nice

he left there
boy ran away
long hair grew
she is lovely
use the car
I forgot it
my favorite teacher
my speech lessons
Dad is older
Christmas in December

make some coffee
I think so
TV is off
can we watch?
what is on?
my old jacket
her friend's name
health is important
school is finished
pizza is delicious

she's my sister
kids were there
where's a chair?
are you late?
he's not hungry
dogs are fun
how's your niece?
use a pencil
lose some weight
start it now

plates are dirty
look outside now
aunt and uncle
they are married
do your homework
I have none
he is handsome
proud of you
can't you see?
take a peek

grow some vegetables
in the garden
I like tomatoes
how was school?
did you learn?
where's her book?
I never go
he needs another
ham and cheese
a big sandwich

Practice Page 4: *Level II*

let me in please
he forgot it now
why won't you talk?
I need my coat
where is that woman?
my class is hard
can you text me?
shirt and pants match
he knows the answer
when is it over?

the lady came here
the clock doesn't work
it's on the couch
can you wind it?
what did you get?
I won't do it
he never comes here
history is exciting
I read the comics
will you talk now?

she is my wife
that is my pen
we need to leave
live in the city
take a long trip
don't forget to pack
I'm very thirsty now
I need a drink
when is the party?
is the girl invited?

who is your nephew?
where does he live?
my favorite CD
I have a computer
it's not on-line
I need more software
the garage is white
be careful of him
the movie was serious
we really enjoyed it

what's on TV tonight?
can we watch it?
I didn't know that
the building closed
I feel very sad
what a great book
who is the author?
my brother left early
she forgot her lunch
can I borrow money?

this is so beautiful
who is your friend?
we are not ready
the house is built
the horses are there
let's go out riding
this is so nice
what did Mother say?
can you stay longer?
this is the end

Stepping Up to Fluency 2. Copyright © 2017 by Janice Pechter Ellis. This page may be reproduced for individual instructional use only.

Supplemental Practice Page 3: *Level II*

what's your name?
close the door
answer the phone
where is it?
do your work
do it now
the brown cat
my new skirt
the open door
why not now?

cut the paper
how are you?
where is Bob?
I am home
never on Sunday
pick any color
what's your number
who is next?
should we talk?
where are we?

shake my hand
eat my breakfast
what's new now?
who are you?
where is it?
a big party
tall thin man
use it all
vanilla ice cream
big yellow ball

small red bow
stop teasing me
sit down quickly
who's my teacher?
what's the reason?
we always come
break the string
take the dog
have some coffee
drink it slowly

when is lunch?
who is coming?
blow your nose
use your head
close the window
turn the knob
small green button
my new ring
use a tissue
which is first?

where's the room?
he is tall
say that again
wash the car
I knew that
can I go?
a yellow box
please email me
need to leave
open the drawer

Supplemental Practice Page 4: *Level II*

why are you here?
we are too late
I broke my pencil
she said she would
where is your father?
I can't see it
the table is broken
this is so pretty
they came here early
he is so tired

what's new with you?
don't forget to call
what a big house!
where is your locker?
has anyone seen him?
here's my bus stop
why won't you dance?
I'm not hungry now
it's time for lunch
don't walk so fast

I like Chinese food
who's your math teacher?
my favorite TV show
the tall, thin woman
did you answer me?
where is my dad?
I like green best
can we wear shorts?
they washed their car
the plant didn't grow

it's eight o'clock now
time for the news
did your sister call?
what did you say?
it's a new suit
which one of you?
it's empty right now
come over here first
I'd like to see it
which movie is it?

can you ride horses?
where do you live?
we went to Mexico
no food is left
where is my magazine?
here's a new towel
do you have money?
why is he crying?
this is my chair
today is really warm

we are too lazy
when is your birthday?
who is your cousin?
please don't do that!
I'm sorry about that
it's blue and yellow
where is the car?
turn the TV off
who is that man?
is this the end?

Multisyllabic Words in Short Sentences: *Level II*

1. I can be *nonjudgmental*.
2. That *autobiography* is long.
3. Some children are *undisciplined*.
4. That song was *unforgettable*.
5. Draw the lines *perpendicularly*.
6. What *entertainment* is provided?
7. I said that *intentionally*.
8. My surprise was *instantaneous*.
9. Her date was *indistinguishable*.
10. *Procrastination* is a vice.
11. Our family is *traditional*.
12. He is a *hypochondriac*.
13. The *experiment* was successful.
14. His illness was *terminal*.
15. Her advice was *practical*.
16. The change was *metamorphic*.
17. We studied the *atmosphere*.
18. He had a *photographic* memory.
19. That was a great *disappointment*.
20. The concert was *delightful*.
21. *Representation* is critical.
22. They received her *application*.
23. Her *conversational* skills needed work.
24. I need *relaxation* daily.
25. She is a *culinary* genius.
26. Please use the *dictionary*.
27. Can we *communicate* better?
28. I enjoy his *personality*.
29. We bought a large *watermelon*.
30. I was *embarrassed* by his actions.

The Final Target
Phrasing

By now, through practice in speech sessions, at home, and independently, clients can consistently say four-word phrases fluently without a model. They are ready to be introduced to the fifth target, *phrasing*, defined as follows:

> **Phrasing** is reading or speaking in groups of not more than five or six words (seven to eight words for Level II clients). Words are grouped together by meaning. Rules for phrasing include:
> - Always stop at punctuation marks.
> - Take a *full breath* before each phrase.
> - Use *easy onset* or *light contact* to begin the phrase.

This target is explained and highlighted on the Target Definitions page in the speech book with the other definitions.

The client is given a story written at an appropriate reading level (equivalent to the client's reading baseline stimulus materials). Excellent reading materials for young clients are children's magazines, such as *Highlights, Weekly Reader,* and *Sesame Street*. Clinicians can also photocopy pages from the clients' favorite storybooks such as *Curious George* and the *Adventures of Frog and Toad*. Older children and young teens enjoy *Scholastic Action* and *Scope*. Popular magazines, such as *People, Sports Illustrated,* or *Time*, are suitable for teenagers and adults with higher reading levels. The story or article selected should be prepared in advance by inserting *phrasing cues* (slash marks to indicate breath groups). Six sample stories with slash marks in the appropriate places are provided (three for Level I clients and three for Level II clients).

The client reads silently or listens as the technique is demonstrated by the clinician. Three or four short paragraphs are read aloud, with phrasing used where specified. After the target is demonstrated, the purpose of the slash marks should be discussed. Clients need to understand fluent speakers read and talk in phrases, whereas stutterers tend to stop and start on every word, giving their speech a distinctive choppy sound.

At the completion of this lesson, the client has been introduced to all five targets in the *Stepping Up to Fluency 2* program.

Phrasing: Determining the Placement of Slash Marks

Additional suggestions for determining the placement of slash marks (phrasing) include:

- Slash before and after prepositional phrases
- Slash before conjunctions separating two phrases and before subordinate clauses
- Slash if a sentence contains more than five or six words without any of the above divisions, using natural semantic units.

Example of appropriately phrased paragraph:

"A long, long time ago, / there was a huge, / scary dragon / in the forest." /

Pauses occur naturally before prepositional phrases. Prepositional phrases often begin with vowel sounds and, therefore, require *easy onset*. *Light contact* is used with phrases that begin with certain consonants.

Phrases also should coincide with punctuation marks, even if the phrase is only two words long (for example, *I will go to the game, / of course, / because my daughter plays / for the team*). This is not necessarily the case when commas separate a repeated word in a sentence, as in *the rabbit hopped, hopped, hopped / down the road*.

The phrasing target can be individualized according to each client's reading and speaking style and needs. If either clinician or client is uncomfortable with the phrasing of a specific phrase, the existing slash mark should either be eliminated or another one added if the client desires a shorter phrase. However, clinical discretion should be used to avoid creating too many one- and two-word phrases. In general, go with what sounds natural for your client.

Practice Page 4 has already prepared the client to make decisions about which targets need to be used within groups of words. The *phrasing* target teaches the same skill, but in meaningful narratives rather than in lists of words. This target also trains the client to group words together that contain a single thought rather than reading one word at a time.

Practicing phrasing requires an entire session after the baseline reading and monologue data are recorded. At least two stories should be completed within a session, for three or four sessions. Six sample stories are included in this manual. These stories feature high-interest content and reading suitable for young children to adult levels. There are three for Level I clients and three for level II clients.

Procedures

Procedures for Readers

Clinician and client take turns reading the selected story. First, the clinician reads one or two paragraphs, then asks the client to repeat the same material. Proceed down the page in this manner. Then, the client reads the entire story independently. Although a copy of the stimulus material is visible, the client should be observed to determine by listening alone (without referring to the copy) the location of each slash mark. The client must pause noticeably, and then begin the next phrase with *full breath* followed by either *easy onset* or *light contact*.

Procedures for Nonreaders

This target can be modified for nonreading clients as follows: The clinician reads each phrase aloud, using all necessary targets, then, asks the client to repeat each one. Even though the client is not reading independently, the clinician listens for the use of specific targets. After going over the story several times, clients may be encouraged to retell it in their own words, using phrasing. Questions should be asked to aid their recall.

First Day of School

Time to get up! / It's 7:00 / in the morning. / It's my first day of school! / I'm in first grade now. / I'm a big _____ (girl/boy). /

I hear noises. / Mom is in the kitchen / making my breakfast. / I'm having oatmeal / and bacon / for my first day / in the first grade. / It's time to get dressed. / I'll wear my new black / and white sneakers / and my favorite T-shirt / for good luck. /

After my hot breakfast, / my mom walks me / to the bus stop. / It's nice and warm outside. / The birds are chirping. / The breeze is blowing. / It is sunny. / Here comes the bus! /

I climb onto the bus / and find a seat / in the front. / This girl looks friendly. / I'll sit with her. / After a short ride, / we pull up to my school. / It's called Acorn Run / Elementary. / I'm happy / but a little scared. /

We all walk / into the school / with some teachers. / I tell them my name. / It is also / pinned to my T-shirt. / One nice teacher / walks me to Room 3. / As I enter, / a tall, kind lady / says she is Mrs. Peabody, / my teacher. / She shows me to my seat. /

On my desk / I see a picture of ME! / How did it get there? / My mom and dad / must have given it / to my teacher. / I feel like I belong here. / I can't wait / to meet the other kids. /

I am ready / for my first day of school. /

— *by Janice Pechter Ellis*

The Petting Zoo

There was a petting zoo / in our home town. / Many nice farm animals / lived there. / There was Lana Lamb, / Gary Goat, / Peggy Peacock, / Davy Duck, / and Pete the Pig. / My favorite was Gary Goat. / I liked his little beard. /

Every day, / many children would gather / around the little pen / to feed and pet the animals. / They could give them / pieces of carrot, / bits of food, / or handfuls of grain. / All of the animals / got lots of attention / from the children. /

One day / there was a new arrival / to the petting zoo. / His name was Larry Llama. / He was taller / than the other animals. / He had big brown eyes, / a very soft nose, / and a velvety face. / He had a woolly white fleece / and a long neck. / The children wanted only to pet him. / He had the longest line / of children / in front of his area / of the pen. /

The next day, / Larry Llama / did not feel well. / He stayed inside the little barn / in the shade. / The children were sad. / All the animals were confused. / They were getting / all the attention / as they had before. / Why weren't they happy? / They realized / that they did not want Larry / to feel sick. / They wanted him / out in the sunshine / with them. / They wanted the children / to love him too. /

After a few days, / Larry was better / and went outside. / Once again the children laughed / and shouted with delight / to see their new friend. / The children paid attention / to all of the animals, / because they really / loved them all. / All the animals / had a nice time being fed / and touched / by the girls and boys. /

The petting zoo / was a warm / and wonderful place / to visit for all. /

— *by Janice Pechter Ellis*

The Lion and the Mouse

Once when a lion was sleeping, / a mouse ran over his nose / and woke him up. / The lion caught him / in his big paw / and got ready to eat him. /

The mouse cried out, / "Please, Mr. Lion, / let me go! / I was scared and lost. / If you free me, / I may be able / to help you one day." / So the lion let him go. /

Some time later, / the lion was caught in a trap / in the forest. / The hunters / tied him to a tree / with a rope. / He could not get free. / He roared as loudly / as he could for help. /

The mouse heard his voice. / He ran to the spot. / He nibbled at the cord / that held the lion. / At last, / the lion was free. /

"Thank you, little mouse," / said the lion. /

"You are welcome, Mr. Lion," / said the mouse happily. /

Moral: / An act of kindness / will be repaid. /

— *from Aesop's Fables*

Level II

The Goose and the Golden Eggs

There was once a man / who had a fine goose. / Every day the goose / laid a big golden egg. / The man sold the eggs. / He was slowly getting rich. / But he wanted to have / a great deal of gold / at once. / He said, / "I wish that I were rich now. / Every day my goose / lays a golden egg. / She must be / all gold inside! / If she is not, / how can she lay golden eggs?" / He said to himself, / "I will kill the goose / and get all of the gold / at once!" /

So one day, / the man killed the goose / and tried to find the gold. / But alas, / there was no gold / to be found. / His goose was like / all other geese. / The man was now / very angry and said, / "I wish I had not / killed the goose. / I wish now / that I still had the golden egg / every day." /

Moral: / He who is greedy / will lose everything. /

— *from Aesop's Fables*

Level II

The Milkmaid and Her Pail

A milkmaid / was on her way to the market / carrying a pail of milk / on her head. / As she walked along the road / that summer morning, / she began to plan / what she would do / with the money / she would receive for the milk. /

"I will buy some hens / from my neighbor," / she said to herself. / "These hens will lay eggs / every day. / I will sell these eggs / to the minister's wife. / And then, / with all of this money, / I will buy myself / a new dress / and ribbons for my hair. / I think they shall be green / for green looks the best / with my long blond hair. / And I will wear / this lovely gown / to the country fair. / I will look so fancy / that all the young men / will wait in line / to dance with me. / I will simply pretend / that I don't see them. / When they ask me to dance, / I will throw my head back / without a care." /

As the girl spoke, / she tossed her head back, and down came the pail of milk, / spilling all over the road. / Her imaginary story / came to an end, / and she began to cry. / The milkmaid was left / with an empty pail / and the knowledge that / she would be scolded / by her parents / when she returned home. /

Moral: / Never count your chickens / before they hatch. /

— *from Aesop's Fables*

Helen Keller

Helen Keller was an American author, / political activist, / and lecturer. / She was the first / deaf-blind individual / to earn a Bachelor of Arts degree. / She is most remembered / by her portrayal / in the film and stage play / *"The Miracle Worker."* /

Helen was born / on June 27th, 1880 / in Alabama. / She was born / with the ability to see and hear, / but contracted an illness / at 19 months, / resembling scarlet fever / or meningitis. / This left her both deaf and blind. / She learned to communicate / as a young child / with the daughter / of the family cook / by using informal "home signs." / By age seven, / Helen had more than 60 signs / to communicate / with her family members. / She learned to identify people / by the vibrations of their footsteps. / She enjoyed music / by feeling the vibrations / of the sound on table tops. /

In 1886, / Helen's mother / contacted Alexander Graham Bell, / among other professionals, / who worked with deaf students. / She was eventually introduced / to Anne Sullivan, / who became Helen's instructor, / governess, and companion / for the next 49 years. /

Helen was determined / to communicate / and spent her life / giving speeches and lectures. / She learned to "hear" / by reading lips with her hands. / She studied Braille / and became proficient with this / as well as sign language. / Helen wrote books on women's suffrage, / labor rights, / and socialism. / She died in 1968 / at age 87. /

She showed the world / that deaf people can survive / and communicate in a hearing world. / She remains / one of the most famous deaf people / in history. / Her birthplace in Alabama / is now a museum. / June 27th is now known / as "Helen Keller Day" / in Pennsylvania. /

— *by Janice Pechter Ellis*

Poems for Phrasing Practice

Use of Poems

Another way to reinforce phrasing is by reading poems aloud. A poem consists of a series of rhythmic phrases, often with rhyme between the lines in each stanza. For many stutterers, reciting poetry is a fluency-enhancing experience, and they look favorably on it as positive reinforcement. Parents of very young children showing early signs of stuttering are often advised to recite poems together with their children to reinforce fluent speech. Therefore, clients may find reading these poems fluently is easier than the preceding stories with phrasing. Poems are provided along with the prose phrasing exercises as a reward for attaining fluency. A client may have been able to read these poems aloud with some degree of fluency prior to intervention. Now, however, the client is using specific fluency techniques actively to achieve fluency rather *riding on fluency.*

Poems of different levels of difficulty are included on the following pages. These poems facilitate use of all five targets. Many of these poems have initial vowel words at the start of many of the lines. This reinforces the easy onset techniques and provides a nice review. Additional poems specific to the client's interests may be used to supplement the poems included in this program. Clinicians should point out the necessity of using all five targets while reading poems aloud.

If I Were an Apple

If I were an apple
And grew on a tree,
I think I'd drop down
On a nice boy like me.

I wouldn't stay there
Giving nobody joy:
I'd fall down at once
And say, "Eat me, my boy."

— *Traditional Rhyme*

Beautiful Things

Beautiful things
I know so well,
Like flowers and trees
And tiny seashells

And sometimes when
I go to bed,
All these things
Pop into my head.

And while I sleep
I dream of some,
And joy into my dreams
Does come.

— *by Janice Pechter Ellis*

Lost at the Zoo

If I were lost
Inside the zoo,
I think that this
Is what I'd do.

I'd say, "Giraffe,
Please look around —
Your head is high
Above the ground."

"Will you point out
to me the place
Where you can see
My mother's face?"

I'm sure Giraffe
Would find my mama,
Looking at an elk
or llama.

I'd leap to her
Like a kangaroo,
And never get lost
Again in the zoo!

"Lost at the Zoo" by Ilo Orleans.
Reprinted by permission from V is for Verse
(Lexington, MA; Ginn and Company, 1964)

I Want to Go Traveling

I want to go UP;

I want to go DOWN;

I want to go traveling

All around town.

I want to go HERE;

I want to go THERE;

I want to see the Circus;

I want to see the Fair.

I want to go LEFT;

I want to go RIGHT;

I want to find acorns;

I want to fly a kite.

I want to go EAST;

I want to go WEST;

I want to lie down

For a good long rest.

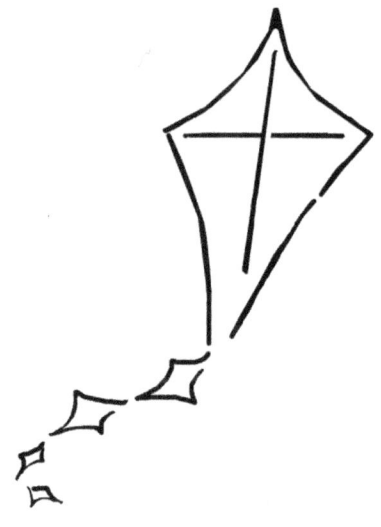

"I Want to Go Traveling" by Ilo Orleans. Reprinted by permission from V is for Verse (Lexington, MA: Ginn and Company, 1964)

Eletelephony

Once there was an elephant,
Who tried to use the telephant —
No! no! I mean an elephone
Who tried to use the telephone —
(Dear me! I am not certain quite
That even now I've got it right.)

Howe'er it was, he got his trunk
Entangled in the telephunk;
The more he tried to get it free,
The louder buzzed the telephee —
(I fear I'd better drop the song
of elephop and telephong!)

— "Eletelephony"
by Laura E. Richards from Tirra Lirra
published by Little, Brown and Company

The Monkeys and the Crocodile

Five little monkeys
Swinging from a tree;
Teasing Uncle Crocodile,
Merry as can be.
Swinging high, swinging low,
Swinging left and right:
"Dear Uncle Crocodile,
Come and take a bite!"

Five little monkeys
Swinging in the air;
Heads up, tails up,
Little do they care.
Swinging up, swinging down,
Swinging far and near:
"Poor Uncle Crocodile,
Aren't you hungry, dear?"

Four little monkeys
Sitting in the tree;
Heads down, tails down,
Dreary as can be.
Weeping loud, weeping low,
Crying to each other:
"Wicked Uncle Crocodile,
To gobble up our brother!"

— *"The Monkeys and the Crocodile"*
by Laura E. Richards from Tirra Lirra
published by Little, Brown and Company.

The Four Seasons

Autumn is a happy time
For children and adults.
Instead of staying in the house,
We frolic like young colts.
We run and jump and play in leaves
Until we're tired out.
And then after we've rested,
We again run about.

Winter is a snowy time
For chipmunks and for squirrels.
They often hide beside the trees
And watch for boys and girls.
They hide their nuts and acorns too
In many different ways.
Their nice fur coats will keep them warm,
While they wait for warmer days.

Springtime is a pretty time
When trees and flowers grow.
The grass is green, the air is sweet,
We see everyone we know.
We want to go outside and play,
We could go to the zoo.
The bears are there, the zebras too,
Perhaps a kangaroo.

Summer is a sticky time
For everyone we see.
We ride a bike, go to the pool,
Might even climb a tree.
Moms keep busy, fathers too,
But children most of all
They want to play all summer long
For soon...it's back to school!

— *by Janice Pechter Ellis*

Fun Limericks

A Silly Bear
A bear who was seeking some honey
Decided first to find money.
So he looked all around,
Including the ground,
And he certainly looked very funny.

The Hairdo
There was a young lady from Maine
Whose hairdo was really quite plain.
So she thought she would curl it,
She cut it and twirled it,
And then she felt pretty again.

The Lucky Man
There was a young man from Kentucky
Who really was feeling quite lucky.
So he bought a new horse,
And he loved it of course,
And then he was feeling quite ducky.

The Diet
There once was a child whose nanny
Just hated the size of her fanny.
So she went on a diet,
She thought she would try it,
And goofed when she ate a banany.

I'm sorry
There was an old woman from Kent
Whose intentions were always well meant.
But she went to the store,
Bumped into a door,
And said "sorry for making a dent."

— *by Janice Pechter Ellis*

Wouldn't it be Funny

Wouldn't it be funny
Wouldn't it now,
If the dog said, "Moo-oo"
And the cat said "Bow-wow"?
IF the cat sang and whistled,
And the bird said "Mia-ow"?
Wouldn't it be funny
Wouldn't it now?

— *Traditional Rhyme*

Use of Intermittent Slash Marks

After completing at least six stories and five poems, using appropriate phrasing throughout, the client should have mastered this skill, taking *full breaths* naturally and using phrasing correctly while reading. Reading material with intermittent slash marks is now introduced.

Clients read these stories aloud without the clinician's model. They are asked to raise a hand at the beginning and end of each section not marked with slashes to indicate when they determine the *phrasing* independently. As they proceed through the entire story, clinicians should give positive and negative reinforcement as appropriate.

Practice for Nonreaders

This portion of the program should be omitted for nonreaders. Instead they can practice using *phrasing* independently with sequential picture cards, as discussed in the upcoming section "Promoting Fluency in Conversation."

Worksheet With Intermittent Slash Marks: Level II

This is the time to introduce Level II clients to "Complex Easy Onset Sentences with Multisyllabic Words for Phrasing." This worksheet combines all five fluency targets with the multisyllabic words practiced previously. Depending on the client's confidence level, these can be read either dependently or independently of the clinician's model. The client is reminded to tap the syllables of the more challenging words in each sentence with the fingertips as they are pronounced. Most clients appreciate the help the slash marks provide.

Following this worksheet are stories with intermittent slash marks. These stories are used for further practice on consistent *phrasing*. The missing slash marks may be added, then each phrase read aloud by the clinician and repeated by the client if needed.

Review

Previous lessons should be reviewed as often as possible with clients, using Easy Onset Sentences, Light Contact Words, or other suitable practice lists. Review is necessary to keep techniques familiar and automatic.

Level I: Intermittent Slash Marks

The Country Mouse and the City Mouse

Once upon a time, / a city mouse named Amos / went to visit his cousin Marty / out in the country on a farm. / Marty was happy / and welcomed his cousin. / He offered Amos food / such as grilled cheese / and peanut butter and jelly sandwiches. /

Amos was used / to eating fancier foods / such as roast beef, / pizza and crab cakes. / He said "No, I don't want this food. / Come with me to the city. / I will show you how to live." /

Amos and Marty set out on their trip. They came to Amos' home and entered the dining room. Crumbs of crab cakes, baked potatoes and pies were all over the table.

The mice were hungry / and very excited. / Before they began to eat, / they heard the scratching of claws / on the floor / and meow sounds. / "What was that?" asked Marty. / "It is only the two cats," / answered Amos. /

"Only?" shouted Marty. "Good-bye cousin," he said, and ran all the way back to his little house on the farm in the country.

Moral: / It is better to be safe / than to have danger / meowing at your door. /

— *From Aesop's Fables*

A Day at the Circus

It was a sunny Saturday. / The Martin family / went to the circus. / As the show began, / Tonya, Paul, Marcy, / and their parents / found their seats / in the big tent. /

They watched / as dogs in little skirts / were jumping through hoops, / riding around in little cars, / and doing other amazing tricks. / There were poodles, / pugs, and terriers. /

Then ten clowns came out into the ring on roller skates. There were big clowns, small clowns, fat and skinny clowns. They had hair and clothing of many bright colors. The clowns made balloon animals and sent them flying into the air. They pulled colorful scarves from their sleeves and hats. They did some magic tricks and made the people laugh.

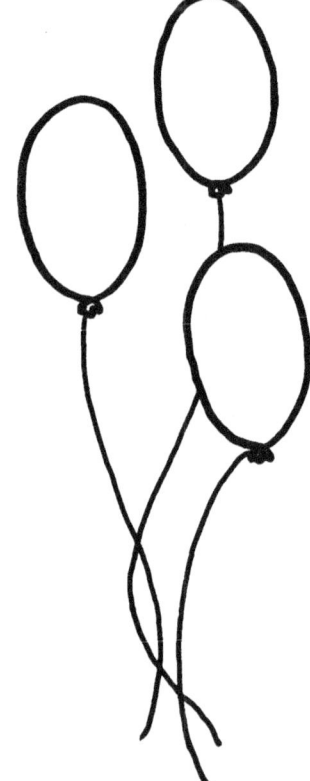

Next the Martins saw acrobats / pedal tiny bicycles / across tight ropes / high in the air. / There were nets / covering the ground / underneath the wires / in case someone lost their balance. / The acrobats would swing / back and forth, / high and low, / sometimes catching each other / in the air. / It was all so exciting / to watch. /

In another ring across the circus tent, Tonya, Paul, and Marcy watched as beautiful lions and tigers paraded around and jumped through large hoops. They seemed to be very well trained. The crowd yelled "oooh" and "aaaah."

— continued on next page

Later, / eight large elephants / clomped out. / They were "holding hands" / by holding trunks and tails / as they walked. / These mighty and beautiful animals / were able to balance / on one foot / or sit up on their back legs / for a moment. / It was all very thrilling. / The people clapped and cheered. /

Mr. Martin / brought the children / cotton candy to eat. / He chose the blue / and the pink flavors. / Mrs. Martin brought cups of soda and popcorn. /

After four hours, the show came to an end. The children had a wonderful time. Tonya, Paul, and Marcy were happy they had seen the circus. They would remember this day forever.

— *by Janice Pechter Ellis*

Level I: Intermittent Slash Marks

The Singing Bone

A long, long time ago, / there was a huge, scary dragon / in the forest. / It was fifty feet tall. / It was as tall / as the highest tree / in the forest. / When it breathed out, / it felt like an earthquake. / It ate all the cows / and sheep / in the village. / It ate all the crops. / It scared all the people. / The king offered a reward / for whomever / could slay this dragon. /

One day, Ludwig and Hans set out for a walk in the forest to look for the dragon and get the reward. They found a cave. It was dark and full of old bones. Ludwig was afraid to go in. Hans was not. He was the brave one.

Hans found a pile of rocks / in the center of the cave. / He called to Ludwig / to come in. / Ludwig then acted brave / and entered. / All of a sudden, / the pile of rocks moved! / It was the dragon! /

Ludwig, the coward, hid behind a wall. Hans picked up his sword and shield. He battled the dragon. He was on the dragon's head. He was up. He was on the dragon's tail. He was down.

What happened next? / Hans slew the dragon. / Ludwig could not believe his eyes. / He came out of hiding. / He went straight to the castle. / He took all the credit / for slaying the dragon. / The king gave him a pot of gold / as a reward. /

Years later / in the springtime, / a young shepherd boy / found a beautiful flower / under a tree / where the dragon went down. / Under the flower / in the dirt / he found a bone. / He carved a flute from this bone. When he blew into it, it played a song / about a man named Hans who slew the dragon. Now the whole world would know about the true hero.

— *Adapted from Grimm's Fairy Tales*

Level II: Intermittent Slash Marks

Complex Easy Onset Sentences With Multisyllabic Words

1. Illegible printing / is hard to read.
2. Illinois and Iowa / are in the midwest.
3. Illustrations of flowers and plants / are helpful when planting a garden.
4. Imposing one's values on others / is inconsiderate.
5. Immerse the broiler pan / under hot sudsy water / to soak.
6. It is inconceivable / that he would miss her wedding.
7. Emphasize her strengths / rather than her shortcomings.
8. Encourage your youth group / to participate in the bake sale / and the car wash.
9. Equilibrium is achieved / when there is a balance of emotions.
10. Evaluations from a supervisor / can make one nervous.
11. *Oklahoma* and *Carousel* / are popular old musicals / by Rodgers and Hammerstein.
12. Osteopathy / is the treatment of diseases / of bones and muscles.
13. Astronomy / would be interesting / to study as an adult.
14. Authorization is required / before entering / that government office.
15. Authentic jewels / are displayed in their natural form / at Natural History Museum/ of the Smithsonian Institution.
16. Apologies / are gratefully accepted / when one person hurts the feelings / of another.
17. Ultraviolet rays are present / in sunlight / and can be harmful to skin.
18. Uncivilized behavior / is not acceptable here.
19. Underdeveloped countries / are still of major importance / to the United Nations.
20. Initial vowel utterances / should always be said / using *easy onset*.

Level II: Intermittent Slash Marks

Benjamin Franklin

Benjamin Franklin / was one of the Founding Fathers / of the United States. / He was a highly renowned author, / printer, postmaster, / scientist, inventor, / politician, activist, / statesman, and diplomat. /

Benjamin was born / on January 17, 1706 / in Boston, Massachusetts. / He came from a large family, / one of 17 children. / He attended school for only two years, / but continued his education / through independent study. / At age 12 / he became an apprentice / in the printing trade. / At age 17, / Benjamin moved to Philadelphia / and worked in several printing shops. / In 1728 / he became the publisher / of the Pennsylvania Gazette. / In 1733 / he began publishing / the Poor Richard's Almanac / under the pseudonym / Richard Saunders. / This became the institution for which much of his popular reputation is based. He wrote countless proverbs, which are often quoted in today's world. Two commonly used are "A penny saved is a penny earned" and "Fish and visitors stink in three days."

— continued on next page

Benjamin was also a prolific inventor. Some of his best known inventions are the lightning rod, bifocal glasses, the Franklin stove, and the glass harmonica. The idea for a public library is also his. He studied and published oceanography findings, including ideas for sea anchors and watertight compartments. He was an avid musician and chess player as well.

In his public life, / Benjamin was the appointed / postmaster of Philadelphia / from 1737 until 1753. / At this time, / he became one of two / deputy postmasters-general / of British North America. / He became the Ambassador to France / from 1776 through 1785. / When he returned home that year, / he became an abolitionist / and freed his two slaves. / He became the president / of the Pennsylvania / Abolition Society. /

From 1785 through 1788 he served as Governor of Pennsylvania. He also served as host to the Constitutional Convention of 1787 in Philadelphia.

Benjamin Franklin's legacy of political and scientific achievement will continue. He continues to be honored by his picture on coinage and the $100 bill, names of places throughout the United States, and cultural references.

— *by Janice Pechter Ellis*

The Shoemaker and the Elves

There was once a shoemaker / who was very, very poor / although he worked quite hard at his trade. / He came to a time / when he had / only enough leather / to make one last pair of shoes. / He cut them out, / and laid the patterns / on his desk. / He fully intended / to make the shoes in the morning. / At that, / he lay down quietly, / and went to sleep. /

The next morning when he arose, to his great surprise he found the pair of shoes ready to be worn! They stood on the table where he had left the pieces of leather the previous night. The shoemaker examined each shoe. They were neatly sewn. They were indeed the work of a master cobbler.

Later that morning, / a customer came into the shop. / He admired the shoes, / and paid a handsome price for them. / The shoemaker was thus able / to buy enough leather / for three *more* pairs of shoes. /

He readily cut out the patterns / for these shoes. / He placed his materials on his workbench, / to be completed early the next morning. / With a contented feeling / about his successful day, / the shoemaker retired to his bed. /

He arose early the next morning, with renewed spirit, ready to begin stitching. Alas! Again he found three precisely sewn, carefully polished pairs of shoes awaiting him at his workbench. His customers were overjoyed at the quality of his work. He was again paid a handsome sum for the footwear. The shoemaker, this time, received enough money for the leather for five pairs of shoes.

Again, he awoke the next morning to find his day's work already completed. This sequence of events continued for several weeks. The shoemaker was soon a wealthy craftsman.

One evening before Christmas, / the shoemaker and his wife / devised a plan. / They decided to find out at last / who was giving them / this marvelous assistance. / So they hid themselves / in the closet / to the right of the workbench. / As the clock struck midnight, / they were amazed to see / three tiny elves sneak through the window. / It was closed / but for a crack. / They at once began to work / on the leather patterns. / They measured, stitched, and hammered / so quickly and expertly / that they were finished / with four pairs of shoes / before the clock struck two a.m. / When their work was finished, / they disappeared as quickly / as they had come. /

The very next morning, the shoemaker's wife suggested that they show their appreciation. They set about making tiny sets of pants, shirts, suspenders, stockings, boots, and caps for the three elves. By evening, these clothes were finished. The shoemaker and his wife set them out on the table where their visitors would be certain to see them. They once again hid in the closet at 11:45 p.m., waiting for the elves to reappear. At midnight, the little men came in and went to the workbench. What a surprise! They picked up the new clothing and put it on. Of course, each item fit perfectly. With a song and a dance, the little men skipped out the window.

The shoemaker and his wife / never saw the three tiny elves again. / Nor did they need to. / From that day on, / the shoemaker had a large business / with lots of wealthy customers / who always paid him well / for his endeavors. /

— *Adapted from Grimm's Fairy Tales*

Level II: Intermittent Slash Marks

Martin Luther King, Jr.

Martin Luther King, Jr. / was born on January 15, 1929 / in Atlanta, Georgia. / His given name at birth / was Michael King, / as was his father's. / His father changed both of their names / after a 1934 trip to Germany / to honor the German reformer / Martin Luther. /

Martin was one of three children. He suffered from depression much of his early life. He had strong feelings about the "racial humiliation" that he and his family and neighbors often had to face in the segregated South.

When Martin was just 13, / he became the youngest / assistant manager / of a newspaper delivery system / of the Atlanta Journal in 1942. / He attended Booker T. Washington High School / in Atlanta, / where he became known/ for his public speaking ability. / During his junior year, / Martin won an oratorical contest / in Dublin, Georgia. / Returning home to Atlanta by bus, / he and his teacher were ordered / by the bus driver to stand, / in order to give seats / to the white passengers. / Martin said, / "this was the angriest I have ever been in my life." /

Martin was a very bright student, and skipped both the ninth and twelfth grades of school. At age 15, he entered Morehouse College, a historically black college. At age 18, he chose to enter the Ministry. He felt that this would enable him to answer an "inner urge to serve humanity." In 1948 he graduated Morehouse and enrolled in Crozer Theological Seminary where he completed his work to become a Baptist Minister. He received his Ph.D. at Boston University. Martin married Coretta Scott in June, 1953. They had four children.

Dr. King became a civil rights leader / early in his career. / He led the 1955 / Montgomery bus boycott, / helped found the Southern Christian / Leadership Conference in 1957, / and helped organize the 1963 non-violent protests / in Birmingham, Alabama. / He also helped organize / the March on Washington in 1963 / where he delivered his "I Have a Dream" Speech. / In 1964, / Dr. King received the Nobel Peace Prize / for his continued work / promoting non-violent resistance. /

His life tragically ended when he was assassinated in Memphis, Tennessee by James Earl Ray on April 4, 1968. He was there planning the Poor People's Campaign, a national occupation of Washington D.C. In 1986, Martin Luther King, Jr. Day was established as a U.S. federal holiday. The Martin Luther King, Jr. Memorial now stands on the National Mall in Washington D.C. It was dedicated in 2011.

— *by Janice Pechter Ellis*

The Fluency Targets Quiz

At this point in the intervention program, an oral quiz on the targets should be presented. No advance warning of this quiz should be given — it should be a surprise. The objective is to see how well the client understands and can explain the fluency targets.

After taking the usual baseline information at the beginning of the session, the clinician tells the client a surprise quiz is being given. The clinician reads each test question aloud and records the client's response. After completing the quiz, the answers — and any errors — are discussed. The quiz is kept in the speech book after it has been scored.

Stepping Up to Fluency 2
Fluency Targets Quiz

What is *full breath*? [2 points]

Name the five targets in order. [10 points]

1.

2.

3.

4.

5.

What is this curve? Explain its meaning. [3 points]

Name at least three sounds that require *light contact*. [3 points]

Explain *continuous speech*. [2 points]

Score:_____out of 20 possible points = _____%

Activities for Conversation, Carryover, and Maintenance

Throughout the training phase of the *Stepping Up to Fluency 2* program, the client's performance on the baseline charts will approach or cluster around the *zero line*. After completing the training phase, the client should have *at least ten consecutive speech sessions* in which disfluency rates for reading and monologue baselines are less than one disfluency per minute before being dismissed from treatment.

Promoting Fluency in Conversation

During these final ten sessions, activities to promote fluency in speaking rather than reading should be initiated. Any language activities are acceptable. Suggestions include:

- Using sequential picture cards for naming and describing
- Playing any board game appropriate for the client's level that facilitates verbalization, such as Guess Who™, Hedbonz™, Trivial Pursuit™, or any other language therapy board game
- Discussion of TV programs, movies, sports, or other topics of interest

Using sequential picture cards is an excellent way to reinforce fluent speech, especially while working on the *phrasing* target. Such card sets are published for different age levels, ranging from young children to adults. For verbalization, the client puts the cards in correct order, takes a few moments to think of two or three sentences about each picture, and when ready, tells the story. If the sentences are too long or unwieldy, the story may be revised aloud. Either the clinician or client can write the story verbatim to keep in the speech book. Several stories can be composed easily within one session.

Verbal games are beneficial because playing them requires speaking aloud. Games should require utterances short enough for clients to remain aware of the targets while playing them. During *all* speaking activities, the goal is for clients to use their five targets to promote fluency while talking. The client needs *plenty of feedback* from the clinician during the activity, such as in the following examples:

- "I liked your continuous speech on that phrase."
- "Did you remember your light contact on the word 'dog'?"
- "Don't forget your full breath before that phrase."
- "I heard a nice easy onset when you began that sentence."

Each session needs to include a variety of activities; a mixture of about 30% reading (poems, stories, and reviewing targets) and 70% language activities is ideal. Clients should be encouraged to share any changes they or others have observed in their speech outside the session or in daily routines (for instance, reading aloud in class, talking with friends, or interacting with family members). Clients need to understand these targets must be incorporated into their everyday life at home, school, or play.

Suggested Activities for Carryover

Clients have now spent at least ten treatment sessions engaged in reading and speaking activities in front of an audience of only the clinician and perhaps one or two other clients. At this time they should be ready for carryover activities. *Carryover* is the stage when they are using all their targets outside the comfortable, semi-private atmosphere of the speech session. Completing a minimum of four and a maximum of six additional carryover activities before dismissal is recommended.

Clinicians have the option of charting these carryover activities. Creating a new Disfluency Rate Baseline Chart for the conversation mode may be convenient. The number of disfluencies exhibited during each specific interaction should be counted and recorded on the chart. Syllable rates are not computed for this stage. An example of this chart is for client K.R. chart no. 2 on page 24.

Carryover Activities for Level I Clients

- ***Hold an Open House or Speech Party***

  The clinician can help the client prepare and address invitations to three friends who are not members of the speech group to join the client in a session of playing games or sharing snacks. If the client is usually seen in a group, the rest of the group may have to be rescheduled. This party is not to resemble the usual treatment group; its only similarity is its location, in the speech office. Using the speech office provides some familiarity in the client's environment.

  During this party, the clinician's role is to provide general supervision and take notes regarding the client's use of targets. After this "open house," the client is given specific feedback regarding use of specific targets. The client's comments and feelings concerning this interaction with friends should be discussed.

- ***Hold a Speech Party in a Different Location***

  If the client experienced success (approximately 90% fluency) in the above activity within the speech office, a second speech party can be held in another location – the cafeteria, an empty classroom, or a corner of a play area. The child may invite three different individuals including one adult, such as the librarian or music teacher in the school setting, should be encouraged. The activity selected can be a board game or an active game, such as playing catch. Spending time with the client following the party to provide and receive feedback is an important part of this activity.

- ***Read Aloud to a Significant Adult***

  The client reads a poem or story aloud to a favorite teacher or other school or clinic personnel. This is arranged with the adult beforehand, so they allow ample time to complete the activity. The client should practice the material chosen with the clinician prior to the official reading.

- *Interview an Adult*

   The client can choose an adult in the school or clinic to interview. This can be very exciting, even to a kindergarten child. In a school setting this person might be the nurse, a cafeteria worker, the librarian, or a favorite teacher. Beginning with a familiar teacher, and then later interviewing a less familiar person, such as the vice principal, is usually a good idea.

   Questions should be prepared and practiced together for one or two sessions before the actual interview takes place. Approximately eight questions are recommended for primary children. The nonreading client can memorize the questions, and the clinician can cue any questions that are forgotten. The entire interaction is timed by the clinician using a stopwatch and any disfluency recorded by number and type, such as one block on "is" or one prolongation of "some." This is helpful for providing accurate feedback to the client after the interview.

Carryover Activities for Level II Clients

• *The Interview*

One important activity, and a good one with which to begin, is an interview. Together, client and clinician can choose a person to interview in the immediate environment. This person can be a fellow client, co-worker, family member, teacher, school librarian, or authority figure, such as a vice principal in a school or a supervisor at work.

Part of the session can be used to discuss and list twenty questions to ask this person in the interview. The questions can be as specific or general as the client wishes. The client may want to study and practice these questions at home and conduct the interview during the next session. Or, the questions can be written and presented within the same session. A third variation of the interview is to surprise the client with the name of a person with whom to conduct an interview in an impromptu manner. This last produces the most tension and anxiety in the client. While the interview takes place, the clinician times the entire interaction using a stopwatch and records any disfluency observed by number and type, such as one block on "is" or one prolongation of "some." This information is helpful for providing accurate feedback to the client after the interview.

Interviewing can be used as many as three times, varying the amount of preparation time and anxiety level provided by the interview. In the public schools, a favorite teacher or coach might be considered for the first interview, then perhaps a librarian or cafeteria worker, and later a vice principal or principal. A similar hierarchy can be developed in other settings.

• *The Telephone*

A second carryover skill, crucial for the client, is to be comfortable using the telephone. Most stutterers are wary of both making and answering calls. Telephoning activities fit well with school, clinic, or private practice programs and may be used as an activity two to four times, depending on the needs and skills of the client.

Client and clinician decide together which type of store to call, such as a department store or restaurant. A set of questions should be prepared for the client to rehearse. The sample questions below work well because they generate short responses from store personnel. Clients should be warned their questions may need to be revised depending on store personnel's response.

Calling a Department Store

1. Appliance department, please.
2. Do you have microwave ovens?
3. What is the price range?
4. Do you carry General Electric?
5. Thank you very much.

Calling a Restaurant

1. Where are you located?
2. Do you take reservations?
3. What are your hours for dinner?
4. Thank you very much.

- ***The Salesperson***
  This carryover activity involves accompanying the client to a store such as a pharmacy, grocery, computer, or appliance store. First, client and clinician work together to prepare a list of approximately ten questions that can be recalled from memory or by glancing at notes. In these settings, the client speaks with the sales clerk one-to-one, while the clinician blends into the background but stays within earshot so specific feedback can be provided later.

- ***The Personal Setting***
  An activity that can be monitored independently without the clinician's presence should be selected by the client. For an older elementary or middle school student, this might be a lunchroom conversation with friends and for adolescents or adults, a specific interaction with a supervisor at work. In this activity the client monitors fluency subjectively and reports about it at the next session. Because this activity is so personal and individualized, it must be developed cooperatively by clinician and client.

These carryover activities are vital to the total success of this fluency program. Nearly all clients achieve fluency within the speech session. This fluency is not stabilized, however, until the client can maintain the use of targets in the "real world."

Maintenance

A maintenance period, rather than just stopping treatment once the carryover phase is completed, is mandatory for all clients to achieve lasting fluency. This is true for both public school students and clients seen in other settings. The maintenance period is necessary to help clients achieve a feeling of independent fluency, while still actively monitoring fluency.

During the maintenance phase, each client should be seen once every three or four weeks, depending on the specific needs to be met. Three months of these follow-up sessions provide a gradual withdrawal from treatment.

> Before clients are dismissed from this fluency program, they should understand they are not "cured" of stuttering, although they can and will be fluent speakers. They must always remember to use the target techniques to retain fluency. They should keep their speech books in a safe accessible place, and review and practice the targets periodically.

Picture Cards

Reproducible picture cards are provided with this program. They consist of six sets of illustrated cards; each set focuses on words beginning with a different phoneme. The sounds featured are [p], [b], [t], [d], [k], and [g]; the words are printed on the back of each page. These pictures are intended for use with nonreaders.

Also included are "Mr. Yes" and "Mr. No." Use of these cards is described on page 125.

pencil	**park**	**pin**
pour	**pup**	**paint**
peanut	**pot**	**pets**
pie	**party**	**pear**

baby	book	banana
buttons	bear	boy
ball	bath	bee
barn	bus	bank

tears	towel	talk
toes	team	time
toad	tire	tent
tall	table	teach

deer	**drum**	**duck**
dress	**doughnut**	**doll**
dozen	**doctor**	**donkey**
dog	**desk**	**dance**

kite	candy	kitten
key	cowboy	comb
call	coins	kiss
car	king	cow

grapes	**girl**	**gloves**
good-bye	**ghost**	**gum**
gorilla	**game**	**goat**
globe	**gas**	**guitar**

Mr. Yes

Mr. No

About the Author

Janice Pechter Ellis earned her Bachelor of Science in speech-language pathology from Pennsylvania State University in 1976 and her Master of Arts in speech-language pathology from George Washington University in 1977. She holds the Certificate of Clinical Competence and is a member of the American Speech-Language-Hearing Association. She also maintains her State of Maryland Licensure.

Janice worked as a speech-language pathologist with Prince George's County and Calvert County Maryland Public Schools from 1977 until 2015. Her students ranged in age from pre-school through high school. She continues to maintain a private practice for clients with fluency and articulation disorders.

Stepping Up to Fluency 2 is her fourth book. She is also the author of *Stepping Up to Fluency* (1998), *Fluency Criterion Program for Young Children* (1988), and *Fluency Criterion Program* (1986), all currently out of print.

www.ingramcontent.com/pod-product-compliance
Lightning Source LLC
Chambersburg PA
CBHW080413300426
44113CB00015B/2501